on being liked

James Alison

A Herder & Herder Book
The Crossroad Publishing Company
New York

For the purposes of conversation regarding *On Being Liked*, James Alison can be reached at **cgfragments@btinternet.com**

The Crossroad Publishing Company
481 Eighth Avenue – Suite 1550
New York, NY 10001

Published in the United Kingdom by
Darton, Longman and Todd Ltd
1 Spencer Court
140–142 Wandsworth High Street
London SW18 4JJ

© 2003 James Alison

The right of James Alison to be identified as the author
of this work has been asserted in accordance with the
Copyright, Designs and Patent Act 1988.

All rights reserved. No part of this book may be reproduced, stored in a retrieval
system, or transmitted, in any form or by any means, electronic, mechanical,
photocopying, recording, or otherwise, without the written permission of
The Crossroad Publishing Company.

ISBN 0–8245–2261–3

Library of Congress cataloging-in-publication data is available.

Phototypeset in 11¾/13½pt Perpetua
by Intype Libra Ltd
Printed and bound in Great Britain
by Page Bros, Norwich, Norfolk

1 2 3 4 5 6 7 8 9 10   06 05 04 03

CONTENTS

Among the many people who have borne me up over the period in which this book saw the light of day, I would particularly like to acknowledge and thank those friends whose names follow below. They have helped as stirrers into action, readers and critics, prompters of ideas, editors of chapters in whole or in part, and sources of advice and information. Without their input this book would be much poorer.

Fr Aldo Tos, Andrew McKenna, Barbara Andrade, Bernard Lynch SMA, Brenda Wall, Brendan Walsh, Brian Davies OP, Carlos Mendoza Alvarez OP, Catherine Shea, Colin Ellis, Revd David Broad, Diana Culbertson OP, Dorothy Walker, Gabriel Andrade, Gerard Loughlin, Fr Gerry Proctor, Revd Giles Fraser, James Keenan SJ, Janice Daurio, Jim W. Davis, John Gerlach OP, John Mathis SSJE, Justin Price OSB, Mark Jordan, Mark Lodico, Mary Grove, Michael Kelly, Paul Ford, Revd Paul Nuechterlein, Philip Endean SJ, Robert Mickens, Revd Robert Wiggs, Sebastian Moore OSB, Susy Brouard, Timothy Radcliffe OP.

And of course, I am once again indebted to the team at DLT who have helped me so much by their enthusiasm and the pleasure they take in their work.

Note on Bible usage
Quotations from the Bible are taken from the Revised Standard Version except where the author has modified the translation to bring out a nuance.

Sometimes we have to freeze the frame. When you read or hear St Luke writing in his Gospel or the Acts of the Apostles, often you have the impression of being treated to a cinema-like picture of something happening. These scenes are so well narrated that we imagine that they took place 'just like that'. And it is no great surprise that St Luke has offered us some of the most memorable scenes to be put into pictures. Think of the Annunciation, the road to Emmaus, the Ascension, the Coming of the Holy Spirit like tongues of fire in the Upper Room, the martyrdom of Stephen. Yet in each of these cases, something much richer is going on than a mere glimpse at a scene. A hugely complex testimony to divine impact in the midst of a human situation is being conveyed with very great economy. Far from saying something 'less' than would be said if it really *had* 'happened just like that', something much more is being said. We often imagine that narrative, or storytelling, is an inferior vehicle for conveying truth which 'just has to do' in the absence of empirical or positive facts. But this is a prejudice which gets in the way of our seeing that empirical or positive facts only reach us at all through being already embedded in story.

So sometimes we have to freeze the frame. I'll ask you to do that with me now. Imagine that you are accompanying St Peter on the road from Joppa to Caesarea to visit the house of the gentile centurion Cornelius.[1] Peter has had this bizarre vision just before agreeing to come. He has been told to eat all sorts of vile and repugnant animals which were forbidden to him by the purity code which he inherited and believed to be from God. He refused three

1. The full story is told in Acts 10.

times, on the grounds that this was clearly wrong. The instruction seemed to be one from heaven telling him to do something which was against God's Law. It would have been perfectly reasonable to see this as a temptation from an evil angel masquerading as an angel of light. The instruction which he received was 'What God has cleansed, you must not call profane.' Yet there was no evidence of God having cleansed anything.

So walking to Caesarea with Peter must have been somewhat disconcerting. He was in a muddle. 'Inwardly perplexed' is what it says. What could this mean? You arrive at the house of Cornelius, still not quite sure what this is about. Peter appears to have worked out that the vision of the unclean animals is something to do with visiting unclean gentiles, since when Cornelius asks him to speak, Peter makes clear that he was happy to come into his house, since 'God has shown me that I should not call any human profane or unclean' – not quite what the voice had said, but a clear sign of how Peter was interpreting it. Cornelius then asks Peter to tell the gathered gentile household all that he had been commanded by the Lord.

Until then, Peter hadn't really been aware that he had been commanded by the Lord to tell them anything. He had assumed, reasonably enough, that all the things concerning Jesus to which he had been witness were for the benefit of Israel and the Jewish people, however widely spread. But it dawns on him that he is being pushed into telling the same story he had told before in Jerusalem, but now to these gentiles. And this is an entirely different context in which to be telling the story. It is a completely Jewish story about how a good man was deemed to be a dangerous and destabilising other and so killed, and yet how he turned out to be the innocent victim who was God himself, come among God's own people so that, in recognising what they had been doing, and in realising that that very ability to recognise is the gift of someone who loves them, they might be set free from their sins. The same, uniquely holy story, born in the midst of God's circumcised and holy people, is now told for the first time in the midst of vile and repugnant, profane others. In order for Peter to reach even this point, he has had to undergo a stomach-churning disorientation of losing the sense of goodness and holiness which came from being separate, first so as to enter their house at all, then to imagine that the story might have anything to do with them.

Peter hasn't even finished telling the story when already 'The Holy Spirit fell on all who heard the word.' This is the maximum moment of being disconcerted. That a holy story should be told to a group of the impure as something confrontational, something to make them feel bad about themselves so that they might purify themselves, maybe even going so far as to seek circumcision, is perfectly comprehensible. Yet, as you watch the story being told you notice that, rather than being confronted and downcast, the listeners all find themselves overwhelmed from within with a sense of delight, seeing the story as good news for themselves. That is seriously weird.

Peter then notoriously concludes, '"Can anyone forbid water for baptizing these people who have received the Holy Spirit just as we have?" And he commanded them to be baptized in the name of Jesus Christ.' In a very short space of time in Luke's storytelling we have gone from something rather like 'You are no part of our narrative' through 'You can be part of our narrative, but only on our terms' to 'Heavens, we are part of the same narrative, which isn't the one either of us quite thought it was and it isn't on the terms set by either of us.'

Well, the frame I would like to ask you to freeze is the frame where the Holy Spirit is falling on the gentile listeners, and Peter is looking stunned, trying to work out what on earth this means. There is much, much more going on here than meets the eye. What looks, in cinematic terms, like a straightforward scene from a pentecostalist or charismatic rally, is in fact a cultural earthquake of immeasurably greater proportions. For the first time what had seemed to be an intra-Jewish story is being told to people who, as they hear it, are interpreting it not simply as an intra-Jewish story, but as something of significance for the rest of humanity. Furthermore, their reception and assimilation of the story is feeding back a quite different sense of what the story is really about to the one who was telling it. He is coming away from this occasion quite taken by surprise at having discovered dimensions of the story he had been telling which had never occurred to him.

But something even weirder has happened: the reaction of these people is a sign that they have suddenly found themselves on the inside of something. Cornelius and his household were 'God-fearers', pious gentiles who were 'fellow travellers' with relation to the Jewish worship of God. They went along with synagogue worship, no doubt impressed by the uncompromising anti-idolatrous monotheism in the midst of the smorgasbord of competing cults available in the Eastern Mediterranean basin. But they did so as half insiders, half outsiders. They agreed that they were impure, second-class citizens in a religious system where first-class citizenship was available by joining a particular race through circumcision. And this distinction, between impure and pure, seemed to be an unalterable part of the package: God delighted in the purity of his chosen people, and hated the impurity of the nations. In the frozen frame we see the dawning realisation that God likes the impure people, that God wants them to be on the inside of God's story just as they are. God is not confronting them to get them to repent, or even inviting them to become something else. God is possessing them with delight, and they are delighting in the being possessed. They are starting to tell a story, which in theory is an impossible story, of how they have come to discover themselves liked by God. And of course, the moment that this 'liking' sinks in, it radically relativises the purity law. That law comes to seem merely something cultural, and not at all something divine, because it is nothing at all to do with God's favour.

Please stick with the frozen frame a moment longer: the richness of this astounding moment in human cultural history is to be found there. The Holy Spirit is creating a new and impossible story in the midst of religious and cultural fixity by enabling both the previously 'impure' and the previously 'pure' to work out a new story, together. It is not that the previously impure are seeking approval. They are not. They just find themselves on the inside of the story, starting to work out what it means. The 'authority' on the 'pure' side finds his world being deconstructed in what must have been a very muddling and painful way before recognising that that deconstruction and that pain was a good thing, come from God, and not a loss of face, or of argument, or of principle. He is at his most authoritative when he comes to be able to recognise that. I doubt very much indeed whether all this 'happened' on one day. But I also doubt that there could be a more succinct and truthful way of telling it than Luke's.

I would like to ask you to stay in that frozen frame for the time it takes you to read this book. I am asking you to share with me the sense of the Holy Spirit falling on the surprised gentiles, who had previously accepted their impure status. And to share with me the sense of the gentiles beginning to tell a story that is theoretically impossible. And finding themselves telling it without approval, and while the authority is still wondering what on earth has hit him, while all his nerve ends are jangling with little voices saying 'No, no, stop them, clamp down, this can't be happening, this is all wrong.'

What I think this book is about is my attempt to find the shape of a new story that starts to emerge when there is a rupture in impossibility. It is theoretically impossible for there to be a Christian story told by a gay man or lesbian woman that is anything other than a somewhat penitential account told by someone who agrees to be a semi-impure half-outsider. And enormous amounts of time and energy are wasted on discussing whether what is impossible in theory really is impossible or not by, for instance, engaging in endlessly inconclusive arguments about 'the real' meaning of this or that passage in Leviticus or St Paul. Well, I am unable to do anything other than bypass this discussion, and instead find myself occupying that impossible space. It is only the manifest sense of that space being occupied which will cause it to become clear that the theory was wrong. It is a much healthier attitude to say 'Yes, I can see how it works in practice, but how does it work in theory?' than to labour away at getting some theory right before engaging in practice!

And of course, when the gentiles started to tell their story, it instantly relativised their position as gentiles, such that being gentile, impure and so on, ceased to be at all important, and the only important thing became being human and a new sort of human 'we'. In just the same way, the moment a gay man or lesbian woman starts to be able to tell the Christian story, and it becomes evident that what seemed impossible clearly is not, the whole gay 'issue' becomes remarkably irrelevant and unimportant, simply the sign of a collapsing taboo. Which is why the really interesting theological questions surrounding the gay issue are not the arguments concerning being gay, but rather the ways in which the gay and lesbian discovery of being Catholic just as we are helps all of us develop a richer sense of the kingdom of God which is coming upon us, and so of the splendour of the Church which is that kingdom's sign. And of course, the moment you look at it in this light, straight people are able to find fairly quickly that this is their story as well, and really nothing to do with being straight or gay. Or, in St Paul's words: 'For neither circumcision counts for anything, nor uncircumcision, but a new creation.'[2]

So, in these pages, I am asking you to dwell with me in my incursion into impossibility. I have discovered that what looked like an impossibility is a fading taboo, and that all the violence which goes along with its maintenance is also fading. And that we are beginning to get hints of a new story, one which is being resisted but nevertheless cannot ultimately be resisted. The new story is able to be told by those for whom the old story is over, while at first the new story is simply incomprehensible to those who are valiantly struggling to make sense of the world within the old story. And thus has it been for every generation, dealing with one 'litmus test' issue or another, since that scene at Caesarea.

This book is not a treatise about anything. If it has worth, it is as a resource for readers to create, and rest in, an apparently impossible space with their own lives. The book consists of three 'triptychs', three collections of three theological essays. A 'salvation' triptych, a 'gay' triptych and a 'contemplative' triptych. First in importance in my own mind is the 'salvation' triptych (Chapters 2, 3 and 4). It seems to me that one of the things that we are still flailing about looking for in the aftermath of the Second

2. Gal. 6:15.

Vatican Council is an account of our salvation which makes sense to us. The old default account, common to both Catholic and Protestant 'orthodoxy' was some variation on the 'substitutionary theory of the atonement'. That is, some version of a tale in which Jesus died for us, instead of us who really deserved it, so as to pay a bill for sin that we could not pay, but for whose settlement God himself immutably demanded payment. Not only does this not make sense, but it is scandalous in a variety of ways. It has been one of the principal merits of the thought of René Girard that at last it is enabling us to scrabble towards a new account of how we are being saved which is free from the long shadow of pagan sacrificial attitudes and practice. So, first of all I engage in a deconstruction of the old sacrificial way of understanding salvation, and the nasty little bits of residue it still leaves, which get in the way of our capacity to tell a properly Catholic story (Chapter 2). However, a deconstruction without helping put something better in its place would be either cruel, or radical posturing, or both. The real question is: how can we understand anew that Jesus is the incarnate Word of God, come among us, undergoing murder and rising again so that we can be unbound from our sin and enabled to live for ever? This is what I begin to re-imagine in Chapter 3 by trying to find a non-resentful understanding of forgiveness, and it leads to what has been for me a hugely difficult imaginative shift: that of seeing 'God wanting us to share in the act of creation from the inside' rather than 'God dealing with sin' as being the central axis of the Christian story. That is where I point towards in Chapter 4. As will be clear, this fleshing out of a more healthy account of salvation is, I think, vital for Christian living as we move into the third millennium, and perhaps the most important bit of unfinished business in our reception of the Second Vatican Council.

The 'gay' triptych is perhaps misleadingly so called. In each of these three chapters I am dealing with a major theological issue which it has become necessary to tackle as I find myself creating a new story of catholicity as a gay man. The first is the issue of truth. Life in the Church(es) over my lifetime has been bedevilled with an inability to talk about these things honestly. Whether I am right or not in what I take to be true in this area seems to me less important than the attempt at honest speech, and the honesty here is not even so much that about being gay: it is about being able to dare to say that 'we have been wrong'. No account of how the Church is right about things can do without an account of how the Church has been wrong about things. In the case both of *Humanae Vitae*[3] and the current consternation related to the gay issue, the defenders of the status quo say that it is inconceivable that church authority could have misled the faithful. At the same time there is a notable timidity on the part of those who clearly disagree, and I suspect that this is because we have yet to develop a courteous and rational discourse about the fallibility of the Church. Infallibility makes no sense at all unless it is a very particular sort of exception in a massive sea of fallibility and there is a realistic way of telling the difference between the two that is something other than someone shouting 'I'm right because I'm right because I'm right.' Chapter 6 is an attempt to get beyond the fears of those who duck behind treating the gay issue as a human rights issue (a 'they' issue) so as to avoid treating it as an issue of truth which requires a first-person narrative (a 'we' issue). It is also my attempt to face up to the challenge of spelling out what it might mean to suggest without loss of catholicity that church authority can indeed mislead the faithful.

After the question of truth, the next logical step is to look at conscience, and in Chapter 7 I try to give a picture of the unbinding of conscience as a normal part of the ministry of the Church. Once again, the occasion is a discussion of the conscience of gay people, but the nub of the issue is the relational nature of conscience and the importance of being set free from double binds. This is something absolutely central to the Gospel and the possibility that the Gospel be, and be heard as, Good News. After I have looked at issues of truth and conscience, the final chapter in the 'gay' triptych, Chapter 8, asks: 'What is it like to live truthfully and with conscience in and as Church?' The

---

3. Pope Paul VI's 1968 encyclical maintaining the traditional prohibition of artificial means of contraception.

sauce, once more, is gay, but the fish is Catholic, and an issue of some moment for all Christians: 'How do we relate to the inevitability of institutional life without being swamped by it and without institutional life insinuating itself into our imaginations as a total, and thus totalitarian, system?' I try to face up to this by defending the thesis, fundamental to Catholic theology, that Jesus founded the Church.

The third triptych, the 'contemplative' triptych, does not appear as three chapters, one after the other. That would suggest that they are 'about something'. They aren't. Rather they are the signs of a sinking into another story, pointers to a shift in understanding, a de-centring of being which is in a sense all that theology and life in the Spirit is about. So I have placed one at the beginning, one in the middle (Chapter 5) and one at the end. These chapters are my attempts to show that the creation of an impossible story about which I talked earlier is not the result of intellectual expertise, moral excellence, storytelling skill or erudition. It is the result of being found in the regard of another whom I didn't know, and as I relax into that regard, finding myself known as I didn't know. The claim is that faith is a gift from someone who wants me to believe that they are good for me, and that this means that it is not so much 'what I believe' but that 'I am believed in by another beyond all imagination, and spoken into being by him', which is the source of all joy and new narrative. These chapters are my invitation to you to share with me in the sense of the Holy Spirit falling on those on whom it was impossible that it fall, enabling us to tell a new story because finding ourselves *liked* in the regard of another. In Chapter 1, I try to set out the key concepts. An analysis of our response to the collapse of the twin towers on 11 September 2001 is the backdrop for my attempt to ask what it means to have our heart, and thus our capacity for vision, given to us by the eyes of another who was God himself teaching us to interpret through God's eyes. What it looks like to receive the divine heart and how this relativises the 'pomps and works' which give apparent meaning to 'this world'. In Chapter 5 I share some of the capacity to tell a punctured story which has come upon me as I have heard the Gospel and become unable to tell a story of myself as heroic and marginal. The heroic and victimary story told by grabbing for an elusive centre turns into a story of receiving a story whose centre is given and not grasped. The ability to cease being manipulative is given by a sense of being assured of being loved. Again it is the story of being given a heart by another and through the eyes of another. I wrap up this triptych with Chapter 9, the final chapter of the book, in which I try to spell out more or less rationally the strange sense of passivity which goes along with discovering with joy that I am the object, the symptom, of someone else's story, but without any diminution or displacement. Here I bring together elements of both the 'salvation' and the 'gay' triptychs within an account of learning to lower resistance to being called into being.

It is not that there is an overarching metanarrative for you to find your way through these chapters. What there is, I hope, is a series of nudges as to what it might mean to dwell in the regard of the Other, to discover a 'we' in the being looked at with love, in being spoken to with words which dare us into being as the shared creation of an unimagined adventure born in the rupture of impossibility.

In the almost two years since *Faith beyond Resentment: Fragments Catholic and Gay* was published, both my publisher and I have been astounded at the volume of highly personal and quite wonderful correspondence which has come in from readers all over the world. What had seemed to me like a shot in the dark was clearly not so, but was responded to by people of all sorts and conditions in a way which gave me possession of the book for the first time. It was as I received the regard of these readers and writers that I began to be able to 'own' my own book, and to dare to think that I might after all have been telling something of the truth. I can scarcely tell you what a gift that was: one of the things that has 'gone with the turf' of being gay (though not, I hope, for much longer) is that of being treated as seriously incapable of real truth-telling. It had been my experience, as it has been that of many others, that when it came to talking about matters gay as though there might be an issue of truth at stake (rather than one of mere inconvenience, bad taste or obsession), those close to me tended to explain me away to myself rather than treat me as a truth-telling subject. The feedback from my readers gave me a first sense of the utter relief of being believed about something that was really important to me for the first time in my life. Anyone who has experienced that relief (and I have heard analogous stories from people whose experience of physical or sexual abuse in childhood was never believed until recently) knows that 'being believed after all' is something very close to the gift of new life. Anything worthwhile in this book is owed to the strength, relief and courage with which those readers and correspondents have empowered me, and so I dedicate to them what is, in far more ways than any of them can imagine individually, their work.

London, *February 2003*

contemplation in a world of violence

insights from René Girard and Thomas Merton

I take it that contemplation is a certain sort of seeing.

I take it from Girard that we always learn to see through the eyes of another.

The desire of another directs our seeing and makes available to us what is to be seen.

In other words, there is no reality 'out there' to be seen. What is 'out there' is already, inescapably, a construct made real by human desire. When, as in most of our cases, most of the time, the other through whose eyes we are learning to see is the rivalistic other, competitors, the crowd, what we see is what is given value by them, and the one seeing it is moved by that desire, and knows and loves with that desire: the 'self' becomes the incarnation of that desire, jostling for security, reputation, goodness, success. Thomas Merton refers to this in a number of places as a sort of collective hypnosis. In this, as in many areas, he is onto the same thing as Girard.

I also take it that when we talk about contemplation in a Christian context we are talking about quite a specific sort of seeing. We are talking about learning how to be given our desire through the eyes of another. The other is Jesus, the Word of God. So, we are being taught to look at what is through the eyes of the One who reveals the mind of God. That is, to be possessed by the mind of God ourselves. By being taught to receive ourselves and all that is around us through the eye and desire of God, our 'self' becomes an incarnation of that desire and we start to speak words formed by the un-hypnosis, the awakening desire of the Creator. In other words: we are being taught to be loving lookers at what is by the One who is calling into being and loving what is. We are being taught to see and delight in what is by the One whose delighting is what gives it, and us, to be.

Let me emphasise this point, taken from Girard, since it is much more important than my fragile ability to practise it, and thus than my fragile ability to be able to yield for you any fruit from it. We desire according to the desire of another. That is to say, the eyes of another teach us who we are by teaching us what we want. I take it that this is a simple anthropological fact of no great difficulty. The only question is: which other? The sometimes peaceful, sometimes rivalistic, always ambivalent desire known in John's Gospel as 'the world', or the entirely gratuitous, peaceful non-rivalistic desire, given us as an entirely sentient, conscious human life history by the Word who reveals God's heart? Christian contemplation is, I take it, the learning of the second regard, the regard of the peaceful other.

Rather than give you a précis of Girard's thought – and there are many available – I would like to try and work through something with you in the light of that thought. There was no notion in my mind when I planned to write this, in August 2001, that there would be such examples of violence and the sacred around us that we would find ourselves living in their shadow by the time I actually came to do so, in October of the same year. But the shadow is now very much there, and this is both frightening and helpful: frightening, since talk has to be much more responsible when we are being tested to look and speak well in the midst of something, a test it is easier to avoid under apparently more peaceful circumstances; and helpful, since it makes much easier the fraternity between Girard's thought and Thomas Merton's when we are able to make parallels between the world of tension and crisis from within which Merton was speaking in the mid to late 1960s and our own situation. I am thinking particularly of

Merton's paper 'Events and Pseudo-Events: Letter to a Southern Churchman'.[1]

So, I am going to risk opening a discussion with you in the light of the events of September 2001, aware that what I say is partial, liable to offend sensibilities of which I am ignorant and so on. I ask you to accept that this is a risky form of discourse, and that if it sparks off strong emotions I may not be able to defend what I say, and those disagreeing may well be right. Certainly, I am an authority neither on contemplation, nor on violence, and these are tentative views, tentatively shared.

First of all, I would like to take us all back in our memories to the afternoon of September 11 – the afternoon, that is, for those of us who were on the eastern side of the Atlantic. What I want to suggest to you is that we were all summoned to participate in something satanic. Now, by 'satanic' I don't mean an over-the-top figure of speech, but something very specific, with very specific anthropological content, something whose very ability to be decoded by us is a sign of its failing transcendence. This is what I mean: some brothers of ours committed simple acts of suicide with significant collateral murder, meaning nothing at all. There is no meaning to the act of destruction caused by hijacking planes full of people and crashing them into buildings. It is not an act creative of anything at all, any more than any other suicide is a creative act.

But immediately we began to respond, and our response is to create meaning. It is our response that I am seeking to examine. Our response was sparked by two particular forces: the locations chosen for the suicide with collateral murder – places symbolic of power, wealth and success (never mind that many of those killed were neither powerful, wealthy or successful); and the omnipresence in the cities in question, and particularly New York, of rolling cameras and a hugely powerful media network which enabled a significant proportion of the planet to be sucked in to spectating from a safe distance. An already mimetic centre, drawing more

---

1. This paper can be found in the collection *Faith and Violence* (University of Notre Dame Press, 1968).

attention than ever towards itself, on that day became virtually inescapable.

As we were sucked in, so we were fascinated. The '*tremendum et fascinosum*', as Otto described the old sacred, took hold of us. Furthermore, we did not come to the spectacle with fresh eyes, as to something entirely new. We came with a script given us by a thousand movies and conspiracy novels of the Robert Ludlum/Tom Clancy genre. It is not original to have noticed that the second plane actually crashing into the tower looked less convincing than it would have done in a film. A film would certainly have made it look much better, produced tension, given it an air of deliberation, rather than that almost whimsical videogame-appearance from off the side of our screens. It is not that what we saw was 'like a film'. We have been taught by films and books, themselves borrowing from and playing to ritualistic constructions of meaning, to see what we saw, and to react as we reacted. Like the novelists and the film directors, we know the ritual.

And immediately the old sacred worked its magic: we found ourselves being sucked in to a sacred centre, one where a meaningless act had created a vacuum of meaning, and we found ourselves giving meaning to it. All over London I found that friends had stopped work, offices were closing down, everyone was glued to the screen. In short, there had appeared, suddenly, a holy day. Not what we mean by a holiday, a day of rest, but an older form of holiday, a being sucked out of our ordinary lives in order to participate in a sacred and sacrificial centre so kindly set up for us by the meaningless suicides.

And immediately the sacrificial centre began to generate the sort of reactions that sacrificial centres are supposed to generate: a feeling of unanimity and grief. Let me make a parenthesis here. I am not referring to the immediate reactions of those actually involved – rescue services, relatives, friends, whose form of being drawn in was as a response to an emergency and a family tragedy. I am referring to the rest of us. There took hold of an enormous number of us a feeling of being pulled in, being somehow involved, as though it was part of our lives. Phrases began to appear to the effect that 'We're all Americans now' – a purely fictitious feeling for most of us. It was staggering to watch the togetherness build up around the sacred centre, quickly consecrated as Ground Zero, a togetherness that would harden over the coming hours into flag-waving, a huge upsurge in religious services and observance, religious leaders suddenly taken seriously, candles, shrines, prayers, all the accoutrements of the religion of death. The de facto President fumbling at first, a moment of genuinely humble, banal, humanity, then getting his High Priestly act together by preaching revenge at an Episcopal Eucharist. The Queen 'getting right' what she 'got wrong' last time there was a similar outbreak of sacred contagion around an iconic cadaver, by having the American National Anthem played at Buckingham Palace.

And there was the grief. How we enjoy grief! It makes us feel good, and innocent. This is what Aristotle meant by catharsis, and it has deeply sinister echoes of dramatic tragedy's roots in sacrifice. One of the effects of the violent sacred around the sacrificial centre is to make those present feel justified, feel morally good. A counterfactual goodness which suddenly takes us out of our little betrayals, acts of cowardice, uneasy consciences. And very quickly, of course, the unanimity and the grief harden into the militant goodness of those who have a transcendent object to their lives. And then there are those who are with us and those who are against us, the beginnings of the suppression of dissent. Quickly people were saying things like 'to think that we used to spend our lives engaged in gossip about the sexual peccadilloes of celebrities and politicians. Now we have been summoned into thinking about the things that really matter.' And beneath the militant goodness, suddenly permission to sack people, to leak out bad news and so on, things which could take advantage of the unanimity to avoid reasoned negotiation.

And there was fear. Fear of more to come. Fear that it could be me next time. Fear of flying, fear of anthrax, fear of certain public buildings and spaces. Fear that the world had changed, that nothing would ever be the same again. Fear and disorientation in a new world order. Not an entirely uncomfortable fear, the fear that goes with a satanic show. Part of the glue which binds us into it. A fear not unrelated to excitement.

What I want to suggest is that most of us fell for it, at some level. We were tempted to be secretly glad of a chance for a huge outbreak of meaning to transform our humdrum lives, to feel we belonged to something bigger, more important, with hints of nobility and solidarity. What I want to suggest is that this, this delight in being given meaning, is satanic. When we are baptised, we, or our godparents on our behalf, renounce Satan and all his vain pomps and empty works. And here we were, sorely tempted at least to find ourselves being sucked up into believing in just such an empty work and pomp. A huge and splendid show giving the impression of something creative of meaning, but in fact a snare and an illusion, meaning nothing at all, but leaving us prey to revenge and violence, our judgements clouded by satanic righteousness.

When I say 'satanic', I mean this in two senses, for we can only accurately describe the satanic in two senses. The first sense is the sense I have just described: the fantastic pomp and work of sacrificial violence leading to an impression of unanimity, the same lie from the one who was a murderer and liar from the beginning, the same lie behind all human sacrifices, all attempts to create social order and meaning out of a sacred space of victimisation. But the second sense is more important: the satanic is a lie that has been undone. It has been undone by Jesus' going to death exploding from within the whole world of sacrifice, of religion and culture based on death, and showing it has no transcendence at all. Jesus says in Luke's Gospel (and it is the title of Girard's recent book[2]), 'I saw Satan fall like lightning from heaven.' This is the solemn declaration of the definitive loss of transcendence of the satanic show: we no longer have to believe it, we no longer have to act driven by its compulsions. It has no power other than the power we give it. The pomp has nothing to do with heaven. It has nothing to do with God.

And this of course was apparent to us as well even, and perhaps

2. R. Girard, *I See Satan Fall like Lightning* (Maryknoll: Orbis Books, 2001).

especially, in our secularity. There was the sort of sacred grief I described, but there were also, mixed up with it, genuine out-bursts of compassion: wonder at the two who jumped out of the building holding hands; a warmth of heart as news emerged of the messages of simple love bereft of any huge religious signifi-cance left on answering machines. At the same time as the sacred violence extended its lure, we also made little breakthroughs of our own into simply liking humans. I don't know how it was for you, and I may be particularly personally insensitive, but I was unable to see anything of the humanity involved while watching the moving images on film, because I am so used to the moving images telling a story in which the people killed are simply stage extras, whose thoughts and emotions and broken families we aren't expected to consider. It was only when reading about the incident in the next day's papers that the human dimension managed to start to break through for me.

And this is the vital thing to understand in any use of the lan-guage of the satanic. It is a failed transcendence. It fails to grip us completely. The unanimity does not last. Even in as strongly religious a society as the United States. Reasoned discussion starts to break out. Penitent questions start being asked. A group of Jews and Catholics went together on the Friday after the 11th to a mosque south of Chicago, and circled it, holding hands, to protect those within it throughout their Friday prayers from any potential violence or abuse. The lie does not command absolute respect. There are already in our midst outbreaks of truth, of non-possessed humanity.

It is this that I would like to look at with you, as we attempt to grapple with contemplation and violence. We were pulled in to a certain sort of contemplation through the eyes of others on 11 September. We were pulled in to a powerful show which taught us to look at the world, ourselves and others, in a certain way, one leading to ersatz virtue, fake communion, violence and fear. But we have in our midst, and have had for nigh on two thousand years, One who is teaching us to look away, so I would like to try with you to see what it means to learn to look at these things through his eyes to see if we can't discover the deeper meaning which those apparently fragmentary outbursts of being human can have.

I have chosen two passages which seem to be particularly appropriate. One a Gospel from the last few days, and another one for Advent. Here is the first:

> There were some present at that very time who told him of the Galileans whose blood Pilate had mingled with their sacrifices. And he answered them, "Do you think that these Galileans were worse sinners than all the other Galileans, because they suffered thus? I tell you, No; but unless you repent you will all likewise perish. Or those eighteen upon whom the tower in Siloam fell and killed them, do you think that they were worse offenders than all the others who dwelt in Jerusalem? I tell you, No; but unless you repent you will all likewise perish."[3]

There is something apparently callous about this. We react to bad news as to a form of emotional blackmail, obliging us to 'feel' for the victims, and be outraged by someone who doesn't appear to feel. But not Jesus. His attention is entirely concentrated on his interlocutors. It is not the events themselves which concern him, but their reaction to the events, and what that reaction says about whose power they are in. We can imagine the excitement of those telling him, wanting a pronouncement of appropriately apocalyptic tenor: the Galileans were not sacrificing at Jerusalem, probably at Gerizim, the rival Samaritan sacrificial site. Maybe this was their punishment from God? But the interlocutors are disappointed. Jesus completely desacralises the event, removing any link between God and what has happened. Any link between morality and what has happened. If we are caught up in thinking like that, then we too are likely to act in ways moved by the apocalyptic other, the god of blood and sacrifice and murder, of morality linked to worldly outcome, and we will perish like them. To ram home his point, he chooses an example where there was no obvious moral agency, no wicked Pilate, no sacrifices of dubious validity: the collapse of a tower – maybe an architectural flaw,

---

3. Luke 13:1–5.

maybe a small earth tremor, the shifting of an underground stream, who knows. Once again, Jesus completely desacralises the incident. It has nothing to do with God. But if we are caught up in the world of giving sacred meanings, then we will be caught up in the world of reciprocal violence, of good and bad measured over against other people, and we will likewise perish. Once again I stress: Jesus will not be drawn into adding to meaning. He merely asks those who come to him themselves to move out of the world of sacred-seeming meaning. What does it mean for us to learn to look at the world through those eyes?

The second passage I want to give you is even more explicit, for it is the passage called the Marcan Apocalypse.[4] Wrongly, in my view, for it is specifically concerned with undoing the apocalyptic world view.

Jesus starts by publicly desacralising the Temple. He takes seriously neither its sacred splendour when standing, nor the apocalyptic meaning to be derived from its being razed to the ground.

> And as he came out of the temple, one of his disciples said to him, "Look, Teacher, what wonderful stones and what wonderful buildings!" And Jesus said to him, "Do you see these great buildings? There will not be left here one stone upon another, that will not be thrown down."

Peter, James and John come to him to ask him when these things will be, and what are the signs – they show, in other words, that they are caught up in the apocalyptic imagination. And, as in the passage from Luke which we have just seen, Jesus commands them to look with different eyes.

> "Take heed that no one leads you astray. Many will come in my name, saying, 'I am he!' and they will lead many astray. And when you hear of wars and rumors of wars, do not be alarmed; this must take place, but the end is not yet. For nation will rise against nation, and kingdom against kingdom; there will

4. Mark 13.

9

be earthquakes in various places, there will be famines; this is but the beginning of the birth-pangs.''

The first instruction is not to allow themselves to be lured or seduced into the apparently sacred world of apocalyptic meaning, not to allow themselves to be pulled by their desire into the world which others will want to create. Any other messianism is false. Wars and rumours of wars have no sacred meaning at all, and the one who is looking at what happens through Jesus' eyes will not be frightened of these things, not driven by them in any way. For they are merely the signs of the collapsing world maintained and reinforced by sacralised violence, and that collapse is itself a sign that something very different is coming to birth. Then Jesus commands them to concentrate on what will happen to them:

> ''But take heed to yourselves; for they will deliver you up to councils; and you will be beaten in synagogues; and you will stand before governors and kings for my sake, to bear testimony before them. And the gospel must first be preached to all nations. And when they bring you to trial and deliver you up, do not be anxious beforehand what you are to say; but say whatever is given you in that hour, for it is not you who speak, but the Holy Spirit. And brother will deliver up brother to death, and the father his child, and children will rise against parents and have them put to death; and you will be hated by all for my name's sake. But he who endures to the end will be saved.''

I am still simply staggered by this passage. For in it our Lord sets out the consequences of not believing in the sacred lie. Those who don't believe in the sacred lie, and say so, who believe in the good news that God has nothing to do with these ever-failing apocalypses, nothing to do with any order based on sacrifice, these people will break the unanimity which is demanded by the sacrificial order, and will therefore be subject to persecution and victimisation by an order that only knows that way of reacting to people, especially people who don't believe in it. This message, divinely guaranteed disbelief in the violent sacred, breaking every unanimity, will be carried to every culture on earth which is founded on the same principles, unstoppable. For it is Gospel. What is even more staggering is what Jesus clearly understands about our paranoia. If we are anxious about what we are to say, if we are concerned to justify ourselves before this apocalyptic order, then we are still too much part of it, our imagination is still too shaded by the 'they who are out to get me' which is part of the apocalyptic view. We are not able to look at those scandalised by us with the clean, limpid, non-accusing, non-persecuted eyes of those whose minds are formed by a different order, whose selves are formed through the regard of an entirely non-judging, non-persecuting Other. If our minds are the mind of Christ, then we will not need to defend ourselves, because the spirit of truth which undoes the sacred lie, the Holy Spirit which makes available to us a wholly benign secular createdness, will be speaking through us. The Holy Spirit is there to empower us to put up with the hatred which is how the collapsing sacred is held together, and it is by our standing up that the new creation will be brought into being through us.

In the next section of the Marcan apocalypse, Jesus desacralises the forthcoming sacking of Jerusalem, again removing from it anything to do with God. All these are things to which one must not pay attention. The final section of Mark 13 is concerned with the reverse of what went before: of what does give meaning. And what does give meaning is something very odd indeed. Jesus uses texts from the Hebrew Scriptures to give a taste of the whole established order of everything being shaken. That is to say: he is happy to use apocalyptic language to reverse the sense of the apocalyptic. For the apocalyptic language, about the heavens being shaken and so forth, refers entirely to worldly happenings, bereft of divine significance. But it is in the midst of them that the Lord will come. And he will come, but in a way that will not be recognised except by those who are being trained to look for him where divine meaning is really given, and that divine meaning appears to be given in the parable at the end:

"It is like a man going on a journey, when he leaves home and puts his servants in charge, each with his work, and commands the doorkeeper to be on the watch. Watch therefore – for you do not know when the master of the house will come, in the evening, or at midnight, or at cockcrow, or in the morning – lest he come suddenly and find you asleep. And what I say to you I say to all: Watch.''

Famously, this parable appears to refer to the events which will follow on a few days later: it appears that the Lord comes in the acts of being handed over which follow. He hands himself over at the Last Supper in the evening; he is handed over by Judas at midnight, by Peter at cockcrow and to the Romans in the morning. The real coming is the very reverse of an apocalyptic appearance: it is the subversion from within of the apocalyptic, and will only be detected by those who have been disciplined to watch, those who have not been hypnotised, sent to sleep by meaning given by the spurious and fictitious sacrificial order of the world. The real meaning, the creative meaning, is the undoing of that from within by one who lets himself be sacrificed by it.

So much for the first part of our learning contemplation in the midst of violence. We are given a very specific and very commanding example of the divine regard: it teaches us to look away, not to be ensnared, to desacralise. It is the very reverse of apocalyptic. But I want to say more. After all, a critical regard is just another regard. I want to say that our contemplation means something more. For the regard I am bringing to your attention, one which we are asked to learn, is not simply an intellectual feat based on a correct theoretical analysis of a situation. My question is this: what on earth is the heart behind the eyes we are being taught to look through? What is the deep desire and motivation? What was it that enabled the human being, Jesus of Nazareth, with his human heart, intellect and eyes, to regard things in this way and so to teach us? The person who says 'God' is describing the question, not answering it. Because the real question is: what does this human regard of Jesus reveal God to be?

I am going to stammer around here, and try to begin to put into words some of my sense of the heart behind the eyes. The heart which I take it we are being given in the degree in which we learn to desire according to those eyes. And I suppose that the word I want to discuss is power, and power desiring something. For what Jesus' words reveal, in Luke, and in the Marcan Apocalypse, and what I take them to reveal now, is what real power looks like. We can only begin to learn to see that power in the collapse of ersatz power. We are tempted to imagine that suicide planes, collapsing buildings, increased security, the unanimity of the rich and powerful, and of course, bombs and more bombs and more bombs, are signs of power. Are creative of a new world order. Shift the tectonic plates of history, and so on. And I am not going to deny for one moment that we are living, and going to continue to live, going to have to learn courage and humility and service, in a world shaped by all those forces. But what Jesus suggests is that all that power is a dangerous illusion. His talk is of a quite different power coming, scarcely noticeably, in the midst of all those things, weaning us off our addiction to the sort of crowd desire which makes that power possible and apparently all-englobing. The power of disbelief in the gods made available by the continuing giving and shaping of creation by one to whom all these apparently powerful things are merely an epiphenomenon, something like a firework display happening in the lee of an erupting volcano, a distraction, dangerous to us, but of no consequence to God, a distraction from the real coming into being of an entirely gratuitous, peaceful, creative meaning, and one in which we are invited to be involved.

Here is my point. Jesus not only taught us to look away, not to allow ourselves to be seduced by the satanic. He also acted out what the undoing of the satanic meant: he was so powerful that he was able to lose in face of the satanic need for sacrifice so as to show that it was entirely unnecessary. We are so used to describing Jesus' cross and resurrection as a victory – a description taken from the military hardware store of satanic meaning – that we easily forget that what that victory looked like was a failure. So great is the power behind Jesus' teaching and self-giving that he was able to fail, thus showing once and for all that 'having to win', the grasping on to meaning, success, reputation, life and so on is of no consequence at all. Death could not hold him in, because he was held in being by one for whom death does not exist, is not even the sort of rival who might be challenged to a duel which someone might win. But if death can only get meaning by having victory, if the order of sacred violence can only have meaning if it matters to us to survive, to be, to feel good, at the expense of someone, then someone for whom it doesn't matter to lose is someone who is playing its game on totally different terms, and its potential for giving meaning collapses.

Here is where I am heading: we can imagine in the abstract something of the power which has nothing to do with death. What is much more difficult is imagining that power incarnated in a human heart and eyes looking at this world. Yet that is what we are talking about. A human heart and eyes so utterly held by the Creator that they speak the Creator's heart about this world. And not just in word, but by a creative acting out and living so-as-to-lose to the sacrificial game in order to undo it, thus enabling creation to be unsnarled from our truncation of it into a violent perversion and trap.

Now this is what I find difficult. The heart, the desire, that wants to do something like that. What does it want? Why should it do it? Why not leave us to get on with it, stuck in our charades, thinking the world of our meaning and our death? In other words, the very fact of distracting us, by word and deed, from being involved in what Thomas Merton rightly called 'pseudo events' suggests a desire for us to be something else. The eye that is teaching us to look away from the lure of the sacred is powered by a heart that wants us to be something else. And we learn our desire through the eye of another. Our learning to see through Jesus' eyes will eventually result in us desiring with Jesus' heart – which is to say, our receiving the mind of Christ, which is how we discover the mind of God.

Jesus not only teaches us to look away, but models what it looks like to live from within the utterly non-rivalistic creative power for which death is simply not a reality. There is a desire in this. A desire for us not to be trapped in death. And this is where I think I'm going – something apparently terribly banal but, I

think, of earth-shattering significance. The person who teaches us
to look away and models for us another way of desiring *actually
likes us*. It is only possible to imagine doing something like that for
someone you actually like. And Jesus is doing it for all of us who
are caught up in the sacred lie – which is to say, all of us.

The staggering thing that this means, for me, is that the most
extraordinary fruit of contemplation in the shadow of the violence
which we are experiencing is this: God likes us. All of us. God
likes me and I like being liked. It has nothing to do with whether
we are bad or good, indeed, he takes it for granted that we are
all more or less strongly tied up in the sacred lie. In teaching after
teaching he makes the same point: all are invited, bad and good.
Those are our categories, part of the problem not part of the
solution, not God's category. God's 'category' for us is 'created'
and 'created' means 'liked spaciously, delighted in, wanted to give
extension, fulfilment, fruition to, to share in just being'. We are
missing out on something huge and powerful and serene and
enjoyable and safe and meaningful by being caught up in something
less than that, an ersatz perversion of each of those things. And
because God likes us he wants us to get out of our addiction to
the ersatz so as to become free and happy.

I want to say something more: behind the word 'like' there is
an astonishing gentleness. The word 'love' which we have vastly
overused can have for us the meaning of a forceful intervention to
rescue us, and we can forget that behind a forceful intervention
to rescue us, which may indeed be how love is shown in a particular circumstance, there is something much stronger, gentler
and more continuous, not dependent at all on needing to rescue
us. This is *liking* us. What I want to suggest is that the word *like*
in all its gentleness is the word appropriate for the extraordinarily
unbothered, non-emergency power we mean by creation. It is that
gentle liking that is the sign of a power which could not be in
greater contrast with the power of the satanic. A power so gentle
and so huge that we are able not to be afraid. In the midst of the
false manufacturing of meaning and frightening power displayed
by the satanic, we are being taught that our being liked and held
in being is at the hands of something infinitely more powerful,

infinitely restful, and we can live without fear. What is being revealed is the power of the Creator. 'Fear not, little flock, for it is your Father's good pleasure to give you the kingdom.'[5] Can I say this? It seems to me that the fruit of contemplation in the midst of the violence which is going on about us, and of which we received a splendid example of a failing attempt at satanic transcendence, is this: as we learn to desire through the eyes of another, so we are given the heart of another, and what we learn is the extraordinarily benign, peaceful power of one holding everything in being, liking and delighting in us, without distinction. So strong, so safe that I am not frightened of a clash of civilisations. Personally, the strongest feeling I have had over the last few months is the quite unexpected discovery that I am no longer frightened of Muslims, and that I like them, and that this is only the beginning of discovering what it will mean to rejoice in them and see them as part of an 'us'. Is this not the deepest act of treachery against the satanic order which was turned on in a part of all our minds and hearts by the events of 11 September 2001? And where on earth will it end?

---

5. Luke 12:32.

unpicking atonement's knots

introduction

Alexander the Great famously solved the problem of the Gordian knot with a sword. He simply cut the thing so that it was no longer there to puzzle people. There is a sense in which any of us could do the same with what sometimes gets called atonement theory. We could do so by making the simple and, although surprising, true, observation that while it is a matter of faith that Christ worked our salvation, there is no fixed Christian understanding of how he worked our salvation. There have been many attempts to describe the 'how', but none has ever commanded the status of immutable orthodoxy. The one most familiar to us derives only from Anselm, thus leaving many centuries in which even the Western Church survived perfectly well without it. I want to suggest that this, our inability to propose a majestatic or magisterial account of how we are saved, is a good thing. However, I want to hold back from Alexander's solution. Grand though it may seem to make the problem disappear by denying that there is a problem, I would like to suggest that any view we have of what our being saved might look like depends on how that salvation is brought about. So, simply to deny that there is a fixed understanding of how Christ worked our salvation leaves us at the mercy of the most common story underlying our salvation, the one in the back of our minds. This story therefore gets to run the whole show of teaching us to imagine the enterprise in which we think we are involved, without ever getting the due credit, or the due examination, or the due critique.

I would like therefore to attempt to exhume the corpse of what seems to me to be the default Western understanding of salvation, coming not to praise it, but more properly to bury it, and doing so by tweaking some of the ways in which it has become tied in with almost every element of our faith, and hopefully unpicking a knot or two as part of the process by which we learn to tell a new, and I hope a less dangerous story about our salvation.

Now please let me indicate what I am not about to do. I am not about to engage in a serious study of what St Anselm really meant in his *Cur Deus Homo?*, which may indeed have been quite different from what became the model substitutionary theory of the atonement. Still less am I to engage in the study of Luther's and Calvin's tightening of what they had received into a penal substitution theory of the atonement. Nor indeed will I examine the post-tridentine theories of the sacrifice of the Mass which may have had very much the same relation to default Catholicism as the Reformers' theories had to default Protestantism.

What I am interested in is precisely not the academic disquisition concerning what these authors really meant, but the much more contemporary task of bringing the old default background music into the foreground, where its almost parodic nature becomes audible to us, in itself a fact of considerable interest: why should we now almost instinctively be able to detect that something is terribly wrong with this tune? Then, however, having engaged in the ritual parody of the object exhumed, I want to say: 'It is not enough to laugh! Acids leak from this dead battery into almost every aspect of how we live our faith. Can we not get a new and living battery, a new, more effective and less dangerous default tune to hum along beneath and in our enterprise of faith?' I am also making a not-so-stealthy bid to win the 'mixed-metaphor-of-the-year' award.

Well, to the default tune. It goes something like this: God created the universe, including humanity, and it was good. Then, somehow or other, mankind 'fell'. This 'fall' was a sin against God's infinite goodness and mercy and justice, affecting the order of creation. So there was a problem. Humans could not, off their own bat, restore the order which they had disordered, let alone make up for having dishonoured God's infinite goodness. No finite

making-up could make up for an offence with infinite ramifi-
cations, and God would have been perfectly within his rights to
have destroyed the whole of humanity. But God was merciful as
well as just, and so he pondered what to do to sort out the mess.
Could he have simply let the matter by, in his infinite mercy?
Well, maybe he would have liked to, but he was beholden to his
infinite justice and honour as well. Only an infinite payment could
do, something which humans couldn't come up with, but God
could, and yet the payment had to be from the human side, or
else it wouldn't be a real payment for the outrage in question. So,
God came up with the idea of sending his Son into the world as a
human, so that his Son could pay the price as a human, which since
he was also God, would be infinite, and thus effect the necessary
satisfaction. Thus the whole sorry saga could be brought to a convenient close: those humans who agreed to cover over their sins
by holding on to, or being covered by, the precious blood of the
Saviour whom the Father had sacrificed to himself, would be saved
from their sins, and given the Holy Spirit by which they would
become able to behave according to the original order of creation.
In this way, when they died, they at least would be able to inherit
heaven, which had been the original plan all along, before the fall
had mucked everything up.

As they say: stop me if you've heard this one before . . .

Now before I start trying to untie some of the knots with which
this theory leaves us I'd like to stress something very important:
I'm not going to examine scriptural texts here. I take it for granted
that it is perfectly possible to find perfectly good scriptural justifi-
cation for every element of the old default story, and that if we
come to Scripture with lenses formed by this tune, we will indeed
read Scripture in its light and confirm that it is the one and only
scripturally based story.

But that is a problem with our reading of Scripture and the
lenses we bring to it. I want to suggest that we imagine that we
have inherited a box of Lego labelled 'bridge' with an elaborate
Lego bridge in it. We don't have the front of the box, so we
don't have a picture of what the bridge is supposed to look like.
We merely have the bridge, and a knowledge that the pieces are

supposed to constitute a bridge. Naturally enough, we convince ourselves that, however often we take the bridge apart, really if we are going to put it back properly, it will look like the bridge we know of old. I would like to suggest that the scripture quotations, about ransom, about 'making him to be sin who knew no sin', and so on, are all perfectly good Lego bits, and that whatever bridge we end up with will include all those bits, but it doesn't have to be put together in the same way as we have been accustomed to putting it together: the fact that we have no picture on the front of the box is not meant to leave us imposing the same old pattern on the Lego pieces. Rather, by not imposing a pattern it encourages us to imagine different ways in which the Lego pieces might fit together to make a better bridge, because the learning how to imagine is itself a vital part of the bridge-building game.

Well, so much for my introduction. Now to some of the knots.

the problem of theory

The first point I'd like to make is that a central problem with atonement theory, regardless of its content, is that it is a theory. By this I mean that, merely setting out an explanation of 'how Christ saved us' in a tidy story such as the one we are accustomed to, runs the grave danger, probably unknown to Anselm, of being hijacked by a modern need for theory. What a friend of mine calls 'physics envy'. I suppose this is the need to get the formula right before we put it into practice, which is quite important when it comes to major engineering works, but less useful when it comes to riding bicycles. The need is linked to the Cartesian world of clear and distinct ideas, based on mathematics being somehow the truest form of truth; anything more narrative, being more bodily and thus more subject to the slings and arrows of outrageous fortune, is somehow unsatisfactory and prone to being an inferior mode of truth-telling.

Well, I merely raise the question of what this tells us about the sort of people we are supposed to be: people who learn first in the head, get our hermetic story right, and then this head knowledge will gradually pass down into our heart and our desires, so that by our head instructing our heart we will put our old desires to death, and push ourselves to desiring new things in line with our story, and thus coming to practise love of neighbour as ourselves: meaning, fitting them into the hermetic story we've learnt, just as we fit ourselves.

I suggest to you that this is simply unacceptable as a model for how any human being in fact learns anything. I suggest that it is more reasonable to perceive ourselves as bodies who are called into being over time by others who are prior to ourselves, taught gesture, desire, sounds by what is other to and outside ourselves, so that we come as imitators to be humanised and socialised bodies over time, and that our capacity for telling a story is a vital, tremendously advanced one, and one which depends on other people. Just as our capacity for having our story modified, without its ceasing to be our story, comes through our interaction with other people.

But this means that it must be part of any story of salvation which we learn to tell that it avoid the dangers of succumbing to being intellectually hermetic prior to practice. It is obvious that no one learns to ride a bicycle by mastering theory and then putting it into practice. We learn to ride a bicycle as very small children by imitating someone who can do so already, at first with the help of stabiliser wheels at the back, and gradually learning to keep our own balance, until we can take off the stabilisers and proceed on our own, but even then we do so within flexible learned public conventions which massively precede us, called 'traffic' and 'the highway code'. So, what I would like to suggest, as we come to look at how we are saved, is that in the first place, we are looking not at a theory at all, but at a gradual induction into a set of practices, including relating to the group into which we are being inducted in a certain sort of way, and including the practice of learning how to use a certain sort of language in a certain way.

What I want to suggest is that this is not something which happens when we master the theory, and is thus a secondary or derivative access to the truth of our salvation, but is itself the beginnings of a possibility of discovering the truth of our salvation and being able to talk about it. It is the being inducted into the practices which equip us to be able to tell a new story as a story discovered through that process of being inducted. It is this that begins to enable us to answer the question of what it means that Christ has saved us. In other words: the process of finding ourselves through narrative, not mathematics, is the most trustworthy form of access to truth, and finally the one our humanity cannot do without.

the problem with the perception of God

My second problem with atonement theory is the perception of God which it enjoins as normative. I mean this in two senses, one obvious, and one less obvious. The obvious sense is that it involves God and his Son in some sort of consensual form of S&M – one needing the abasement of the other in order to be satisfied, and the other loving the cruel will of his father. Or another way of saying the same thing, perhaps slightly less provocatively: there is no way that the theory could work without some element of retribution, which presupposes vengeance. Well, I wonder whether this could be shown, but I suspect that over the long haul this element of necessary retaliation, stubbornly held to by many who profess our faith, has done more to contribute to atheism among ordinary people than any number of clerical scandals, and that if being a believer means believing this, then it is better to be among the non-believers. It is a relapse by us gentiles into a form of idolatrous theism which pious Jews of the post-exilic period would probably regard themselves as having left behind some time previously.

But it is the *less* obvious sense in which the perception of God that the theory enjoins is a problem, which I consider more important. I suggest that what the theory does is to make a process of revelation impossible. For if we follow it, it makes out that Jesus' resurrection didn't reveal anything new at all. It merely accomplished a deal whereby someone who was remote and angry remained remote and angry, but created an exception for those lucky enough to be covered with the blood of his Son. Before, God was a hurricane, and now God is still a hurricane, but Jesus has revealed that there is an eye to the hurricane, and so long as you hang in there, in the eye, you won't be destroyed. But, I want to suggest, this is not the case: Jesus' resurrection did reveal something which was new – not new to God, but new to us. Jesus revealed that God had and has nothing at all to do with violence, or death, or the order of this world. These are *our* problems and mask *our* conceptions of God, of law and order and so forth. In fact, God loved us so much that God longs for us to be free from these things so as to live for ever, with God and each other, starting now. Furthermore, Jesus' resurrection revealed this to us, not as part of a magic trick, but as a development of a progressive clarification as to who God really is which had emerged in the life of the Jewish people over centuries. In short: we are recipients over time of an extraordinary piece of Good News concerning God, God's non-ambivalence and God's non-involvement in death and violence, and this radically affects the whole of our under-standing of social order. But atonement theory shortcuts the possibility of our being recipients of revelation over time, short-cuts the process of the apostolic witness and the transmission of faith, and instead of a God whose process of revelation is part of the way God loves us, substitutes an *ex abrupto* disclosure of a secret deal, whose terms we must learn so that we don't fall out of its conditions.

the problem with sin

My third problem is atonement theory's account of sin. This also has two dimensions. The first is that in the story I have told you, sin, not God, is the central character. It is rather as though Rosen-crantz and Guildenstern had taken over a performance of *Hamlet*, as if the story was all about them. You can tell this by the fact that once sin has come into the story – at the fall – all the other characters are reduced to dancing around it, wondering what they should do about it. Well this means that sin runs the story. All the other characters are reactive in one way or another. And of course it is the non-reactive character who is the real god of the story, while the other characters, being reactive, are none of them god. I guess it is no surprise that in a world formed by this story-line, evil should become fascinating, while good becomes boring.

Nevertheless it is the second problem with sin which seems more important, and this is that the storyline as it stands depends on our having an independent source of knowledge as to what sin is, prior to and independent of any knowledge of salvation. That is what the story as we have it postulates: first there was sin; this needed saving from. A salvation was needed which was at least as big as the mess that needed saving; it was provided. We are saved, end of story. However, and this is vital: we have no such independent source of knowledge as to what sin is. It is not as though there were a Jewish doctrine of original sin prior to Christ: there isn't. The doctrine of original sin is a distinctively Christian doctrine, and *pace* witticisms about it being the only Christian doctrine that doesn't need demonstration, it very certainly does! It is the doctrine that the human condition is only accidentally, and not 'naturally' bound in with death. And this is a perception of being human, as being one who was not made for death and need not fear death, which came about strictly and only in the aftermath of Jesus' resurrection. For it was this which revealed, for the first time definitively, what it means that God has nothing to do with death, and nor need we. In other words, sin is only and always a term that is ancillary to, secondary to, and dependent on, an understanding of salvation. Or, to put it more bluntly, the definition of sin is 'that which can be forgiven'. Even psychologically that is true: any non-abstract discussion of sin is for us always the result of some 'aha' moment: 'Oh, so that is what I was doing, and now I see it as falling short of what I am becoming, and so must move on, never doing it again, and trying to undo the harm which I did.'

This links in to my earlier point about God: just as the atonement theory's picture of God makes a process of revelation impossible, so its depiction of sin sets us up to have prior and objective access to something outside any process of which we are the recipients, and then leaves us with a formal forgiveness which is not part of the sort of breaking of heart, contrition or compunction, which is what happens when someone undergoes the process of being given a bigger heart by some one who loves them and wants them to have and to be much, much more than we seem ready to settle for.

This leads in the long term, which means it has already led, to my fourth problem with atonement theory.

the problem of morals

This is the interaction between atonement theory and morals. I would like to suggest that one of the results of our subcutaneous bewitchment by the storyline I set out for you is that it both reduces Christianity to morals and yet makes penitence impossible, with the result that others must bear the weight of my morality. Let me explain: if the problem was that we sinned in the beginning, defecting from some perfect created order, and that fall set up this whole ghastly rigmarole whereby someone had to come and pay the price, then, once he's paid the price, really the only important thing is that we now behave according to the original perfect created order, for if we don't, we are showing that we are not grateful for having been saved, and that we are thus not grateful for that terrible bloody sacrifice which happened on our behalf. Of course, this reduces the preaching of God's love for us to preaching a form of emotional blackmail – 'Look what I did for you – and you still want to make me suffer?' – and thereafter the only thing that matters is our showing our gratitude by conforming to the created order reflected in the commandments, i.e. morals. And what is the history of Christianity, especially in the English-speaking countries, in the last several centuries if it is not the gradual reduction of Christianity to morals? And usually to sexual morals, since these can be codified and reduced to acts and commandments in a way in which, for instance, dealing with markets, finance and group violence cannot.

Yet the storyline does not only reduce religion to morals, it makes penitence impossible. For someone who, following this storyline, allows themselves to be saved by the precious blood, their sin, being part of the abstract package in which they were involved through Adam, is pre-packaged, and forgiven as a package. Thereafter they must just not sin, but hold fast to what is right, and what is right is, naturally, what was always right from the beginning. The trouble with this is, of course, that it completely bypasses the process of the breaking of heart in which we discover for ourselves, as part of real attitudes and patterns of heart and behaviour in our lives, how we are sinfully involved, and what we are really called to be. And it means that someone who is 'other' to us can only be perceived as a threat to our goodness, to which we are now holding, and which is God's original goodness, rather than the point at which my own too-small-goodness can be punctured by someone having access to my vulnerability, and thus allowing me to be made bigger. The 'other' becomes someone to be seen as a threat, to be controlled, if possible, or maybe sacrificed, because, after all, however little we may want to, we've got to uphold what was always true and right and just from the beginning, or else we are denying the efficacy of the sacrifice ('Why would I have come and been sacrificed for you if being "other" wasn't what I've come to save you from?'). And this puts us back into the emotional position of an Abraham who does indeed sacrifice Isaac ('I'm sorry, I've just got to obey this mysterious command'), or a God the Father who is awfully apologetic about this sacrifice business, but unfortunately he can't help it, because there just is the matter of the infinite divine justice and honour to be satisfied. It's not surprising that a barbarous misreading of the Aqedah, the story of the binding of Isaac in Genesis 22, is so often not far from the surface of the storyline of atonement which I set out for you. And this of course means that it is the 'other' who gets to stagger around the world as a sinner, bearing the weight of 'my' morality. It's not pretty.

the problem with creation

And so to my fifth problem, the picture of creation which emerges from the storyline. It is of course a storyline in which creation itself has become a subsection of morals, for the only place for creation in the story is as the reference point for righteousness. This leaves creation as something which happened 'in the beginning' rather than being a permanently contemporary relationship between God and everything that is. It thus leaves us at the mercy of a Deist view of God, coinciding with the perception that sin is interesting, good is boring, and only morals matter. By linking creation and morals in this way (morals are how we live the objective truth about creation which we should have been living all along but didn't because of the fall), a particularly terrible shortcut is produced: creation becomes something 'gone back to' rather than an adventure in which we are invited to participate. And what is worse, the very possibility of natural law, which I take to be simply indispensable to any Christian understanding which refuses to separate our creation and our redemption, falls prisoner to a trap. Instead of natural law being part of the way in which we as humans learn, over time, and indeed collectively, to discover what and who we really are, as part of our process of becoming, natural law becomes something into which we must be coerced as a result of an a priori deduction from a starting point to which we in fact have no access, nor could ever have ('what we would have been like if it hadn't been for the fall'). It is a perversion of this sort and the circularity of the arguments which it engenders which do more than anything else to discredit the idea of natural law. And the link between the a priori version of natural law and atonement theory has not, I think, been sufficiently attended to. In short, with atonement theory, the possibility of our discovering our Creator as our Father over time in a process of coming to discover ourselves as created and as children, invited to participate in a deeply benevolent adventure not of our own invention, is severely compromised.

But how would it be if, in fact, rather than the order of atonement 'logic' being followed, in which first there is a creation, then there is a fall, then there is an irruption of salvation, we were to follow what I like to call the order of discovery: it is from a certain sort of irruption in history that we come to see ourselves as in the process of being able to be forgiven, which is how we have access to participating in the process of being created. This seems like a much more plausible way to tell the story of the Jewish people, and also to tell the story of its extension among the gentiles, up to and including ourselves, recipients, way down the line, of something massively anterior to us, for whom revelation is never a simple disclosure of information, but always received as a process of discovery.

the problem of power

My sixth problem with atonement theory is to do with some of its implications about power. And this is linked to its role as a 'theory'. Any story that can be told without being undergone runs the risk of being too powerful to be compatible with the Christian Gospel. And the atonement theory can be told without being undergone: it enables someone to be right without also becoming someone different. Or, to put it another way, to preach and bear witness to salvation without in fact undergoing salvation. And what sort of salvation is it that can be preached and witnessed to without being undergone? When I say the story runs the risk of being too powerful, I mean that since it can be told by those who have not yet learned how to live as powerless in the eyes of the world, it can be told by people of power, and thus become what I think sounds grander in French than in English: a 'discours du pouvoir'[1] – please either forgive, or giggle at, my lapse into the preferential option for academic grandiosity. Now the thing about a 'discours du pouvoir' is that all sorts of words like 'good' and 'bad' and 'sin' and 'salvation' get to mean what they mean from the perspective of those who have power. But, if the Gospel means anything, it means that the real story told by the crucified and risen victim and his followers, whatever else it may be, can never be a 'discours du pouvoir' in any ordinary sense, because it is a story learned in a process of despoliation, or self-despoliation, of earthly power, so as to receive the power of one who was so powerful that he was able to lose to the powers of earth so as to teach us that

---

1. A 'discours du pouvoir' is a way of talking from a position of power such that the person talking isn't aware of the extent to which what they say is coloured by their own position of power, and consequently they are unaware how far from objective their definitions are.

we too needn't be trapped in their game, and can learn to lose as well, so as to be given something on a scale no 'discours du pouvoir' could imagine.

the problem with group creation

The final problem with atonement theory which I would like to look at here is its relation to group formation. By being a theory which is right independently of practice, of charitable and liturgical involvement, it is very easily able to become an idol in the sense in which it encourages group formation of the good around something which is sacred. Those who adhere to it are 'in' and those who don't are 'out'. If you hold to it, you are covered by the sacrifice, and if you don't, you aren't. I note here that that which is true of traditional evangelical protestants as individuals who make profession of the 'sound' atonement doctrine of salvation, is often also true collectively for a certain sort of traditional catholic in the way they regard the Church: the 'in' individual and the 'in' group are 'in' in exactly the same way. And part of the problem with being 'in' is that it is dependent on there being those who are 'out'. In other words, as with any form of pagan sacrifice, the sacrifice works by helping to create and shore up group barriers.

But this, of course, is exactly the reverse of the sense of Christ's death and resurrection, which, from the beginning were perceived to have been a 'sacrifice' only in the sense that they undid the whole world of 'sacrifices', putting them to an end for ever. Indeed, no clearer sign of that can be given than the way in which, far from creating a new 'in group', the whole meaning of the death and resurrection of Christ was to break down the most significant of group barriers, that between Jew and gentile, and then all other such barriers, slave and free, and so on in ways we know ourselves to be faithful in extending as we discover them. Now here is my problem: not only does the standard atonement theory thus prevent us from sharing in receiving a new identity which has no over-against, the identity of the penitent who are receiving their identity from the victim. More than that, by preventing us from learning vulnerability with the 'other' – that is,

learning who is our neighbour – it leaves us with a particularly
difficult problem: it sets up Christianity in such a way that the
'Jews' will always be the outside other, a group of stage-deicides
necessary for the smooth working of the sacrifice. There is an
implicit anti-Semitism in it, and the fact that the dominance of this
understanding of salvation in Western Christianity from Anselm
to the late twentieth century coincides with that glorious patch of
history which runs from the Crusades to the Holocaust ought
perhaps to give us pause for thought. It seems to me that, whatever our account of salvation and of Christ's death, if it means
that it tends to create a group to which the Jews are not accidentally, but necessarily, an outside other, then it cannot be an
account of the salvation which God is working for us through
Christ.

I end with this, for now, because what I hope to have done is
merely to have shown how deeply the acids from this dead battery
have corroded our motor, and what a lot of work we have to do
to come up with a way of talking about salvation which enables
us, for instance, to read the texts of the apostolic witness without
a deep background distortion to our lenses. Just try to imagine
what it might mean to read St Matthew's Gospel without any of
the pre-formed convictions that lead us to read it anti-Semitically
– as, for instance, an extraordinary development of Judaism,
extraordinarily Jewish in its self-critical capacity to become universal, and in becoming universal, able to be trapped by groups
less subtle than the one which gave it birth into being read over
against those who gave it to us, but also able not to be so read!

So I hope I have at least suggested just how much hangs on our
learning our way through the pitfalls of atonement theory, how
pervasive its influence is in our contemporary Christianity, and
how important it is that we learn to receive a narrative understanding which is in no way dependent on vengeance. Nothing
that is dependent on vengeance can be called reconciliation.

My next task will be an attempt at a particular approach to this
narrative understanding. I will try to set out the beginnings of an
anthropology of forgiveness, which I understand to be central to

what a new story might look like, and see how that enables us to imagine reconciliation.

re-imagining forgiveness

introduction

I'm going to change key a bit. In comparison with the confident and schematic approach I adopted in the last chapter, now I am going to shift into a more tentative voice. I want to struggle in your company with a dimension of the understanding of Christ's work of salvation which I think gets short shrift in a faith corroded by atonement theory. This is, to put it provocatively, a search for a rigorous anthropology of forgiveness.

I'd like to start in a personal space: with a nagging doubt with which I'm left in the wake of my recent book *Faith beyond Resentment: Fragments Catholic and Gay*. My attempt in the book had been to create a space within which gay people might learn (and eventually, following the dictum that a preacher is the last to hear his own sermon, even I myself, might learn) what is meant by being able to forgive those who hate us and what is meant by becoming free from resentment towards those who persecute us. In other words, a fairly straightforward attempt to understand those key parts of the Sermon on the Mount as they apply to gay and lesbian people.

Yet might it not be possible to say: 'It's all very well trying to be beyond resentment, but isn't the mere act of presenting some sort of public offer of forgiveness in reality a rather subtle form of accusation? Might it not in fact be a particularly clever form of vengeance to offer such forgiveness, a sanctimonious way of telling people that you hope they'll see the error of their ways?'

Well, I'd like to leave aside whether or not that is an accurate description of *Faith beyond Resentment* – an author has of necessity only a rather limited field of vision of his own work, and this author can only say that if the characterisation is accurate, then I have been found wanting where I most hoped not to be. But I would like to treat the nagging doubt about whether or not forgiveness is a particularly clever form of vengeance as the very interesting theological point which I think it to be.[1] It is, to put it into a nutshell, where Nietzsche and Girard clash. And where Nietzsche and Girard clash seems to me to be the place where theology is being forged. So, I would like to use the nagging doubt as a launch pad from which to work out with you whether forgiveness is possible, what it looks like, and why this must inform our intelligence of salvation.

In the first place, let me say where I think the nagging doubt is quite right: to *tell* your persecutors that you forgive them and hope they will one day see the error of their ways is a kind of retaliation — is in fact a claim to the moral high ground, and as such is part of the world of violent reciprocity and identities formed over against each other which, I take it, make the kingdom of heaven impossible. What is interesting is that it is the fact of *telling* them that you forgive them which is the act of retaliation, and as with all such acts of retaliation, most obviously those done by someone weaker against someone stronger, its principal effect is on the one retaliating, not on the one being retaliated against. This means here that its principal effect is on the one forgiving, not on the one being forgiven.

Thus we have the situation, which I suppose any of us can recognise, that there is a certain sort of petulant self-appropriation in the act of a retaliatory telling someone that I forgive them. This telling of a persecutor that I forgive them leads indeed to a form of self-righteousness, and it does so in three interlinked ways. In the first place, in the act of telling I am asserting a sort of counter-factual power, making a claim over against the persecutor, and

---

1. I am particularly grateful to Gerard Loughlin, whose review of *Faith beyond Resentment* in the *TLS* no. 5154 (11 January 2002), p. 28 raised this question in a succinct and exact form, thus sparking off the meditation which led to this chapter.

that claim is saying 'I completely reject you and where you come from, so completely that I am able to turn round and not hold it against you. I am not run by the same things as you are. So, however weak my position looks, I can in fact be as outside your world of values and attitudes as God, and as such can pronounce forgiveness at you.' Now please note that here the pronouncement of forgiveness is the parting shot of an act of hermetic self-enclosure into sanctity. And that is linked to the second sense in which the act of telling a persecutor that I forgive him or her is a form of self-righteousness: it is a way of cutting a bond and turning my back on the persecutor: it is saying 'I am not like you. My forgiving you is my way of saying that I will no longer be contaminated by you.' It is, in short, going off in a huff while extending a sanctimonious mask of godlikeness towards the persecutor. The third sense, linked to this, is that it appropriates the place of the victim: the sanctity of the position of the one forgiving is the claim that as the victim, I am holy and godlike, and my being able to forgive you depends on my being absolutely and unambiguously identified with this holy figure: in short it is a claim to have transcended ambivalence and ambiguity and thus to be a form of the imposition of truth.

In all of this, it seems to me that the Nietzschean suspicion that forgiveness is simply a mask for insipid resentment and is the ultimate weapon of the losers is quite right, and should be insisted on. I wonder also whether it doesn't cast an interesting light on atonement theory and its social effects. For if this is what telling someone they are forgiven is, then the decree of forgiveness which was the result of an extraordinary backroom deal between Father and Son emerges, with Jesus saying 'Father forgive them, for they know not what they do' as merely a resentful expression of divine weakness sanctimoniously expressing a grudge against the ongoing power and brutality of the world. And it means that the role of the clerical caste in maintaining that forgiveness becomes one of living out this resentful expression of sanctimonious weakness on behalf of the sanctimonious victim who pronounces forgiveness, but never ceasing to be parasitical on the brute power which has to have forgiveness helplessly pronounced at it.

Now I would like to begin to explore with you why I think that the Nietzschean suspicion, while a very proper critique of atonement theory, does not in fact exhaust what is meant by either forgiveness or salvation. In order to do this, I would like to stick within the terms of reference of the scenario set up by my book, *Faith beyond Resentment*, which at least on the surface might be interpreted to be about gay and lesbian people who are learning to forgive, and others who are persecutors, apparently a simple inversion of the power structure, so that divine weakness is now 'forgiving' hateful worldly power as a particularly exquisite form of accusatory vengeance.

Let me approach this from a slightly different angle. At the time of the Jubilee,[2] in the year 2000, the Holy Father offered apologies on behalf of the Church to various different groups who had suffered at the hands of organised Christianity over the centuries. The various outrages mentioned were, as I recall, a very long time ago. At the time a number of gay and lesbian people spoke up, saying: 'Well, he's apologising to the Jews, the Muslims, the slaves, the Galileos. In fact just about everybody you can think of who was around 500 years ago, except us.' This exception was driven home by the Vatican's own goal in its handling of the Gay Pride march held in Rome that summer.[3] So the same people went on to say: 'Well, why doesn't he apologise to us?' Now I thought at the time, and think now, that this is a silly question, and I think the Roman curial authorities were right not to have apologised to gay and lesbian people. And this is not because there is not a lot to apologise about, but because an apology without a change of heart is a lie. And those authorities have not had a change of heart.

---

2. The 'millennium' celebrations were known in Catholic circles as the Jubilee, or Holy Year.

3. The Vatican managed to persuade the city authorities not to allow the Gay Pride march to follow its own long-planned route through the city centre, claiming that the whole thing was an affront to the Holy Year pilgrims. At the same time, neither the Vatican nor the Rome city authorities were able, for reasons of the Italian constitution, to prevent a neo-fascist party conducting a political rally urging hatred for gay people, along the same route as had been forbidden for the Gay Pride march.

What those who made the demand that the Vatican apologise miss, I think, is an understanding of forgiveness, and how it works. They seem to think that forgiveness works in the 'if . . . then' mode beloved of blackmailing parenting: 'If you say sorry, then I'll forgive you.' In other words the power of forgiveness holds out the reward corresponding to what is effectively a demand for self-abasement. We are all proficient, I have no doubt, in the cosmetic self-abasement needed to flatter those who make such demands from us: it is a question of jumping through hoops, and has of course no relation at all to forgiveness or penitence.

However, in the most traditional framework of theology, for-giveness precedes confession. And the form which forgiveness takes in the life of a person is contrition, that is, a breaking of heart, a deep shift in attitudinal patterns of the sort: 'Oh my God, I thought I was doing something good, or at least normal, and only now do I begin to see that what I was doing was deeply sinful against God and profoundly hurtful of my neighbour, and thus of myself. I must undo in as far as I can what I have done wrong, and make sure never to do it again.' This breaking of heart is eventually received as an extraordinary gift, that of being given to be someone else who I didn't know myself to be and who is much bigger and more splendid than what I took myself to be. That is what forgiveness looks like in someone's life. The actual verbal confession, the apology, or the asking for forgiveness, comes way down the line, and is usually a sign that the person is already receiving forgiveness.

The answer then to those who shouted at the Vatican demanding an apology for their treatment of gay and lesbian people is not, as they seem to think, 'Shout louder, they may hear you and be ashamed' but, I'm afraid, the sadder answer: 'They can't apologise yet, because they haven't yet received forgiveness.' And this brings us back to the nagging doubt with which we started off, whereby a simple pronouncement of forgiveness by the one who has been persecuted would be a form of weak retaliation dressed in sanctimony. So, assuming that the hard-hearted haven't yet received forgiveness, and that this is why they are hard of heart (or from their perspective, that of course they haven't been forgiven, because their admitted severity is an heroic defence of the divine will in the midst of a hedonistic, godless, relativist, materialist etc. etc. world), how can they be forgiven? And what would that forgiveness look like? And who will forgive them if it is not those whom they have hurt? And if it is the ones who have been hurt who must forgive them, must not that forgiveness be displayed as gentle perseverance in the face of incomprehension and being dismissed long before it bears the fruit of enabling contrition in the heart of those becoming able to receive forgiveness? And is not, as in the sacrament of penance,[4] the actual pronouncement of forgiveness by the forgiving victim the crowning of a process that began long before, in awkwardness and confusion, and thus a word spoken in response to, and confirmatory of, the flowering of a new being in the one being forgiven? And is it not the case that that pronouncement of forgiveness is actually creative of a new 'we' between forgiven and forgiver?

Well, I come to it this way, but many of you will come to exactly the same perception through other routes. I rather think that this, very exactly this, is where we begin to be able to start to talk about our salvation at the hands of Jesus Christ in a way which gets us out of the coils of atonement theory, and yet enables us to give the lie to Nietzsche's objection to forgiveness.

I have given examples from both sides, that of the one forgiving and that of the one being forgiven. These show what does not work. So now I would like to make the move which I hope to be strictly of the Gospel and try to struggle with you towards a necessary shift of perception so as to find what does work.

If the temptation of those who consider themselves to have been hurt by forces far more powerful than themselves lies in some sort of sanctimonious retreat into victim status, casting forgiving curses at their former adversaries, and yet the perceived task is to be not just cosmetically, but really forgiving 'from your hearts',[5] then I suspect that the first step in this task is to go through the effort of coming to see oneself as a recipient of forgiveness: in short, not

---

4. More popularly known as 'Confession'.
5. Matt. 18:35.

someone who is primarily a victim and secondarily a forgiver, but someone who is primarily forgiven, and for that reason capable of being a forgiving victim for another, without grasping onto that, or being defined by it. This is a huge emotional and spiritual task, but without it, we will not, I think, understand the salvation which we are receiving from Christ.

What this looks like in the examples I have given, is coming to see oneself as part of the unrepentant hard-hearted block that is in need of forgiveness, and starting to imagine oneself as in the process of being forgiven, which means re-imagining how that process of forgiveness reached us first, re-imagining it as something done 'for us' and coming to meet us, and as it meets us, enabling us to be turned into imitators of it, so that we may be the same to others just like ourselves. All I am trying to do here is to recover the anthropology behind a phrase like St Paul's

> Why, one will hardly die for a righteous man – though perhaps for a good man one will dare even to die. But God shows his love for us in that while we were yet sinners Christ died for us.[6]

> But God, who is rich in mercy, out of the great love with which he loved us, even when we were dead through our trespasses, made us alive together with Christ.[7]

However, I am trying to recover that anthropology in such a way as not to fall into any of the traps of atonement theory which I tried to set out in the previous chapter.

So, let me now try to have a first go at telling the story of Christ in such a way as to give us an understanding of salvation which is purely gratuitous, without any element of retribution, and in which forgiveness is a divinely initiated process lived out for us in our midst with a view to making us participants in something bigger than we are.

I'm not going to try to tell the whole story, but just the central

---

6. Rom. 5:7–8.
7. Eph. 2:4–5.

part, the crucifixion and resurrection, since it is they which enable us to advance in this conundrum. I take it that the resurrection is the making available to us of the crucifixion as the forgiveness of sins. In other words, it is a reaching into the hardest part of our hard-heartedness, where our involvement with death is most complete, in our tendency to hold on to life at the expense of victims, and think we are just to do so. By giving himself to that mechanism of ours, and there appears to be no human culture or society that we know of that is not dependent on it in some way, Jesus was allowing himself to *lose* to it. Now please note this. That what we have been taught so often to regard as a victory looked in fact, for all the world, like a defeat. It looked not as though Jesus conquered sin and death, but as though death, our human mechanism by which we are involved in death, conquered him.

Now I would like to ask you to consider the sort of power involved here. If two rivals are more or less at the same level of power as each other, let us say, two armies, or two tennis aces, then the result of their rivalry will be the defeat of one and the victory of the other, or in some particularly awful cases, the defeat of both, each preferring mutual destruction to allowing the other to win. We call it a victory when one of the near-equals in such a fight wins over the other. However, when there are not two nearly equal partners, as for instance when a young parent and a young child are playing tennis, we are in a different world. For the parent to play with the child as if they were near equals would be a catastrophic dereliction of parenting, for to insist on beating the child as if they were genuinely rivals would be to produce a terrible rivalry in the child, a real stumbling block to the child's growth. The more normal pattern would be one of two sorts: the parent teaching the child to *win* or the parent teaching the child to *play*.

In the first case, the parent is going to adjust him- or herself to the level of the child's strength, and gradually play with the child harder and harder so that the child's strength and skill level grow by practice over time. The parent is never going to humiliate the child by beating them unduly easily, but nor are they going to let themselves be beaten, because what they want the child to do is to want to win. This means having the competitive edge constantly sharpened. Here in fact the parent is modelling a desire to win by constantly holding the prize of winning just outside the edge of the child's possibility, so deferring satisfaction, thus getting the child wound up to be a really hard competitor.

In the second case, we have a parent teaching the child to *play*. This will mean, as in the first case, being a sparring partner for the child at the level of the child's strength, but also learning the even greater skill of actually being able to lose without patronising the child. This way the child gets to experience the satisfaction of winning and at the same time learning that he or she doesn't have to win. That the game is about playing, an end in itself, and for that to be possible, rivalry must have its limits, must be capable of being indulged in for the purpose of having a game at all, but also must be sat loose to, must be capable of being suspended for a higher cause.

I hope that it is clear that the modelling of desire in which the parent is engaged in the second case is a far richer one than that modelled in the first. And the key to its being far richer is the parental ability to lose in just the right way. That, I would like to suggest, is the real meaning behind Jesus' self-giving up to death. He was able to lose to those who had to win, so as to enable them, by not having to win, to be able to play.

What I would like to suggest is that this 'being able to lose' is the result of a far greater power than the power of beating a close rival. Because being able to lose is the power of one who isn't a rival at all, but likes the one he is playing with so much that he wants them to be able to lose as well, not so as to humiliate them, but so that they might be set free from the compulsion to win in order actually to enjoy playing.

Now, I suggest to you that Jesus of Nazareth, incomprehensibly to those surrounding him, went voluntarily and with considerable freedom to his death in just this way, losing to the human need to survive-by-creating-human-victims, in order to show that no one ever need create victims in order to survive again. This raises the question of the sort of power that he had, up to and including his death. If this story of salvation is true, then the sort of power he had was the power of the one who knows not death, for whom death is not something with which he is in rivalry, in short, it was the power of God. I think that this is what is meant by the doctrine of the Incarnation: after the resurrection of Jesus made available what his life and death had been about as forgiveness, the apostolic witnesses began to be able to perceive that what had enabled Jesus to give himself up to death was that he was already deliberately involved, as a terrestrial human being, with a set purpose, making of his death 'a losing to death' so that we could be shown that we too can live as if death were not.

Now please note that this 'losing to death' was not done so as to 'please the Father', but rather so as to get through to *us*. It is we who could not be unhooked from our addiction to death until we were shown that we could live as if it were not. So Jesus' going to death was not something acted out, yes in our midst, but with the Father as prime audience. It was something acted out by the Father empowering the Son to give himself for, towards, at, us. Not only *on our behalf*, but, as it were, *in our face*. It is we who need to be weaned off our addiction to death and to having our beings formed as though the end of our biological lives were our enemy.

The resurrection then would be the breakthrough into our world of perception of something which had not been perceivable before, that God has nothing to do with death, and that humans need not either. And the consequences of living that out would start to be born: that we can gradually, ourselves, learn to live as if death were not by, in a variety of ways, undergoing death beforehand so that it loses all power over us, and we start to be able to live free of its compulsions. I take it that the blessedness, or happiness, of the blessed in the Beatitudes is precisely owing to their being able to live as if dead in the midst of the world. Time and time again in Paul this is talked about as the primordial Christian experience: undergoing a form of dying-in-advance so as no longer to be driven by death in our living.

Well, I would like to ask you to consider briefly here how this all feeds into an understanding of forgiveness. If I am at all right in the hints I am getting of an anthropology of forgiveness, what

I am talking about is the very specific and exact way in which 'the Son of man has authority on earth to forgive sins'[8] and how we are supposed to be multipliers of that power.

My suggestion is this: that what forgiveness looks like is an ongoing process, again and again, of learning to behave as if death were not, which will mean coming gradually to stand up against those whose being depends on death, and running the risk of being persecuted by them, and maybe even killed by them. In other words, we as addicts are recipients of someone loving us in such a way that he wanted us to be free from our addiction, when we didn't even know we were addicted, and he chose to set us free from that addiction by making it visible to us that we no longer need live in that way, and that our very being can be unbound from being formed by death. In the degree to which we start to behave towards others in the same way, so we are set free.

Now, here's the point: forgiveness in this model is precisely not a hermetic self-sealing off from the other whom I declare myself to be nothing at all like. On the contrary, forgiveness turns out to be a creative moving towards someone *whom I am like* in such a way that they will be free from death *with me* so that together we will be a new 'we'. It is not a simple gesture or a pronouncement, but a living towards running the risk of being killed by the person, over time. And what is the reverse of the self-separation of the Nietzschean suspicion that we saw is that if someone moves towards me, and comes to live out my sphere of addiction over time, in order to reach out to me, even if they are in no way moved by my compulsions, by the mere fact of living in my universe they begin to become like me. And by the simple fact of occupying a position of apparent powerlessness within my sphere, they invite me to begin to become like them: they after all occupy the space which I myself am most frightened of occupying, the one to the avoidance of which so much of my energy is dedicated.

If this model is true then consider the following: as a human, Jesus was allowing himself to become like us. In fact, the allowing

8. Matt. 9:6; Mark 2:10; Luke 5:24.

himself to become like us was not a reactive thing, but a creative one: he decided to become like us, which involved not merely physically losing his life so that we might lose our fear of death, but losing his human identity over time, in forgiveness, so that we might be given his identity, and he ours. I can think of no better way of acting this out than inventing a mime in which you give your body to people and tell them to repeat this over time. Nor can I think of a better way of making sense of John's talk of Jesus having to go so that we might receive the Holy Spirit.[9] This is God agreeing to share his human identity with us over time. If you want another example of this, at one remove from our Lord's own acting out, then consider his instruction to his disciples: 'Behold, I send you out as sheep in the midst of wolves; so be wise as serpents and innocent as doves.'[10] Rather than this being an instruction about prudence, as it is usually made out to be, I suggest that this is what acting out forgiveness in the world looks like. It looks like knowing that you are dealing with dangerous people, who are more than likely to be deeply destabilised by your innocence and because of that to seek to lynch you. You forgive them by living with them with the twin attitudes of the wisdom of the serpent, knowing very exactly how to slither away to avoid being trampled on when danger is around, but the innocence of doves, who do not think ill of those whom they are seeking to forgive, nor are in any sort of rivalry with, but are able to give themselves 'sacrificially' as it were to the addicts, having the power to make of it the best show they can.

I think that this means what we in fact all instinctively know, that the spreading of the Gospel and the creative living out of the forgiveness of sins by those for whom death is no longer a form of compulsion to be embraced or avoided are the same thing.

When I say this is a creative act, I know I am talking about something rather difficult. But this is key. For if I am right in interpreting the resurrection as the making available of what God wanted for us all along, which involved us becoming unhooked

---

9. John 14:28.
10. Matt. 10:16.

from our involvement with death, then it is not the case at all that forgiveness is to do with our slates being wiped clean so that we can be fitted back into a pre-existing model of creation. On the contrary: forgiveness is our access to being created in the first place: it is the undoing of a temporary hitch on our way into becoming sharers in God's life. This has a particularly important consequence for our Christian life and teaching. It means that forgiveness ceases to be something moralistic to do with how I must have my will bent before another, or a weak decree of forgiveness before an impenitent monster. Forgiveness becomes instead the straightforward objective way by which any of us can be created. It is only by a process of undergoing 'being undone' from various traps, dead ends and ensnarlments that any of us can be brought into being. There is nothing particularly shameful about this: it's just the way it is! And while it may be experienced by any of us who are undergoing it as particularly special to us, which it is, it is also true to say that there is nothing particularly special about it, just as there is nothing particularly shameful: it is just what being called into being looks like for human beings coming from where we're coming.

Furthermore – and here I am making a suggestion that I don't have the time or space to follow through – I would suggest that forgiveness is a vital human intellectual tool. It is as we forgive and are forgiven that we come to see what really *is*. It is our way out of being formed by paranoia, which leads to conspiracy theory, and I want to suggest that conspiracy theory is precisely the mindset of those who haven't received forgiveness and who can't forgive, and can therefore not come to perceive what is. But it is in the degree in which we learn to step outside conspiracy theory, of a universe peopled by forces which are militating for or against us, that we begin to be able to learn what is: when we stop believing that a witch, or the neighbour's evil eye, is responsible for the sudden hailstorm which destroyed our crops, then we start to be able to imagine meteorology. Again, I don't think it is by accident that John describes the Holy Spirit as a counsel for the defence opening up to us all truth, things which we couldn't understand yet.[11] The opening up of truth about what *is* happens to us socially as we are able to receive forgiven, non-paranoid minds.

My final point before going back to my starting place is this: if the central image of the power being used is of one so huge, because it has nothing to do with death, that it is able to lose to the forces of death so that we might no longer be captivated by death, and if that power is so huge that it is not a retaliatory tit for tat against a wicked other, but a real power at a level beyond the ken of that distorted other which refuses to see that other as something to be retaliated against, but something to be undone from within, then it is quite clear that victory is at least a highly inappropriate image to use, leaving aside its analogical use in the New Testament. Victory is the language of the near rival who triumphs over a near rival. But from the point of view, if we may use such terms, of the power that is not part of the same universe, a victory *over* someone is not a victory at all. It is in fact a sign that all there is in the universe is conflict and comparative strength.

From the point of view of one who is in no way bound up by death, and is therefore able to imagine and desire the good of the other even as the other maltreats him or her, the only conceivable 'victory' is one in which no one triumphs over anybody else, but all the participants are reconciled as equal. In other words: victory from the viewpoint of the powerful loser is, and can only be, reconciliation, the creation of a new 'we'. Even to want to turn tables on the wicked, apparently powerful worldly other is to be part of the same worldly power as them.

Now, let me take this back to where we started: with the nagging doubt about whether the silken glove of forgiveness is but a clever disguise for the iron fist of vengeance, and my observations about those seeking a papal apology for the mistreatment of gay and lesbian people over the centuries. I hope it has become possible to imagine what it might look like for gay and lesbian people to forgive their persecutors in a way which neither falls foul of the trap of retaliatory self-enclosure into sanctimony, nor

11. John 14:26; 16:12–14.

leaves us demanding an apology which is unlikely to come until those concerned have been forgiven. I also hope that it is by analogy clear that the same possibilities of re-imagining salvation as forgiveness leading to reconciliation apply in quite other fields than the one in which it has been given to me to try to spell it out.

If this is true, then we find ourselves embarked on a dangerous adventure of allowing ourselves to become forgiveness in imitation of the one who gave himself for us, long before we knew we needed forgiving. And this is not an adoption of a moral high ground, because, far from any sort of separation from those in violence, it involves sticking with them, inhabiting their universe, being in their world but not of it, being as wise as a serpent and as innocent as a dove, but always, by not being afraid to lose anything, being prepared to be sacrificed rather than collude in violence. Thus the one forgiving comes to occupy the place which is most feared by the violence, and if it can be lived without fear, it will destabilise the violence completely, and enable those wielding it to be set free from fear, with the result that we together, who do not really know what we are, or what being right really looks like, may come to discover what really is, for that is what we are invited to become, together.

And this, of course, leads us straight into the question of what 'creation' really means, which we will look at in the next chapter.

——◄○►——

creation in Christ

introduction

The order in which the great panorama of Christian salvation is traditionally unfolded is the order which I call the order of logic. We begin with creation and the fall, we move on to salvation, and from there to heaven. As the last two chapters have shown, I am unsatisfied with this paradigm, since I consider that it leads to a series of distortions. I would like with you to try to reconfigure the panorama in the light of what I call the order of discovery. That is to say, I consider that what is first in the order of our knowledge is an intuition of salvation, first worked out and elaborated over many centuries of ups and downs by the Jewish people, which issues forth into a very special refinement of this Jewish discovery in the life, death and resurrection of Jesus. It is starting from this intuition of salvation that a critical understanding of creation was worked out, and not the other way round. Furthermore this relationship between salvation and creation can be detected not only among the apostolic witnesses, but the same relationship can be found even in the texts of the Hebrew Scriptures prior to the first century.

The reason for insisting on this is as follows: if we consider salvation as 'fitting in' to a story which starts with creation, then we remain stuck at the mercy of an a priori view of creation by imagining that we have some independent way of knowing what happened 'in the beginning'. An independent way of knowing which does not pass through the always contemporary here and now of our interpretative capacity. That is to say, we fall into the same mistake of imagining that we have some prior access to what creation is as we saw when we looked at the substitutionary theory of the atonement. That theory imagines that we have a prior and independent access to what sin is. That prior knowledge of sin is necessary for our Lord's death to have made a real difference by wiping it clean. 'The world is a mess, Jesus is the answer' only works if we know in advance what sort of mess it is that Jesus is supposed to be the answer to.

What in fact happens following this logic is that we set up a scenario whereby up to a point we are disposed to learn, to receive, something new, a divine revelation. And then, at a certain point we say: 'No, now I must make an extraordinary mental leap. Now I must jump outside this process of reception which allows me to understand and interpret things, and I must become like God, an external viewer of the whole process, and from this outside position I can dictate the sure norms which must regulate the Universe whose rules I can understand.' That is to say, I erect something sacred. And there, where I erect something sacred, very soon I discover enemies who are undermining the sacred, seeking to knock it down so as to install their perverse and heterodox ideas. And of course, I completely lose sight of the fact that I am as much inside the process of learning now as I was before, though imagining myself outside of it. But now my way of being inside the process of learning takes the form of a dramatic fight with those who are as much inside a process of interpretation as I am, but whom I have wanted to deprive of legitimacy by my insistence on a non-negotiable sacredness. That is to say, I've managed to create a scandal. And being in every way as modern as my opponents, I convince myself that I am speaking from an invulnerable pedigree. I call as witnesses to this process the debates concerning Darwin in the nineteenth century, or the current struggle of the so-called 'creationists' against those who believe in some form of evolution in certain states of the United States and other places.

Well, no. It seems to me very important that we go back to considering the doctrine of creation starting from an understanding of salvation, which is where it comes from. I am going to do this by means of a series of points, still not yet very well linked among themselves, since this is for me a study still in process, which is opening up horizons that will lead I do not know where. For that reason it is a privilege to be sharing with you in what I hope will be a way for all of us to advance in our understanding. So, I am going to proceed by sketching out a series of theses.

we always start from where we are

My first thesis is that we always start from where we are. When Catholics say that God created the universe, we are not making a claim about a 'religious' way of describing how things came into existence. We are not making any sort of claim about a process of *how* things came into existence. We are saying something about our contemporary wonder at the fact that they came into existence at all. We are in fact saying something about our relationship of being brought into being and held in being by God. We are expressing amazement at the gratuity of it all.

This expression of amazement at the gratuity of it all is not an alternative scientific explanation of anything. It is, on the contrary, a condition of possibility for us not to be frightened of advancing as far as we possibly can in our understanding of how things came to be. Being able to trust the goodness, the 'not out to get us' nature of what we will discover is no less important than the intelligence used in asking the right questions about how things came to be, but the two are not conflicting areas of research. The ability to perceive the innocent indifference of what *is* as just that: innocently indifferent, is an extraordinary breakthrough from our normal understanding of power and, more specifically, our understanding of that which is more powerful than us. For our normal understanding of power relations easily detects the play of rivalrous and contradictory desires in our societies, and is inclined to make us think that we need to protect ourselves, or 'they' will get us, or 'there won't be enough' or 'it's all running down'.

So we make a real mistake if we consider creation to be something which very specially has to do with the remote past. The gratuitous nature of there being anything at all is an entirely contemporary perception for us, just as it would have been entirely contemporary with whatever we discover to have been the story of the process of our origins as humans and as universe. Our access to creation is present, as is our access to the past. In other words (and forgive me the obviousness of the point), the only access we have to the past is the access for which our present understanding equips us. We have no access to our origins which is independent of our current interpretative capability.

Let us imagine that someone had filmed the origin of everything, from outside. Well it's self-evident that if someone filmed it, the capacity to film would have been prior to the 'origin' and we'd have the problem of working out where the capacity to film had come from. What is worse, we'd only be able to understand the film in the light of what we can understand now. In the same way, our understanding of meteorites and astronomy is an absolutely contemporary understanding, and one which depends on a whole series of things: investigative institutes, societies which are willing to spend a huge amount of money on the search for such an understanding, and societies which regularly reject the possibility that the discovery of things yet to be imagined could be a crime against something sacred. But it also depends on the refusal to believe that capricious gods, or angels, or djinns, are somehow involved in introducing freak elements into what we discover, such that no rational understanding is possible.

Both the contemporary holding on to a sense of wonder or mystery that there is anything at all, and the contemporary refusal to accept specifically 'religious' accounts of how things came to be are central to what we are talking about when we talk about creation. And of course, the ability to do those things, to hold on to that mystery, and to refuse religious shortcuts, let alone the ability to do both of those together, are abilities which have been acquired over a long time, and have a history.

our growing understanding of the perception that we have been created has always been dependent on the overcoming of violence and death

My second point is as follows: the fact that we speak of creation at all is not something self-evident. The question 'Where did all this come from?' is, without doubt, a very ancient question. But it has always been asked and answered within the scheme of power and order which was in force at the time. And it couldn't have been otherwise. There is no thinker, however brilliant, who is not a child of their own era in at least very many of the things which they take for granted, and from within which they work out their change of perspective.

Yet we imagine, somewhat obstinately, that the most ancient accounts of the origins enjoy a superiority concerning what they describe compared to our own, because of having been closer to the original events. As if they were witnesses to a murder. Of course those who are present at a murder scene are witnesses in a way in which people from later generations will never be, leaving on one side the complexities of interpretation which arise immediately, for of course it is possible that two eyewitnesses can differ enormously in what they describe, and that a later interpretation made, for instance, by a lawyer during the trial of an alleged murderer, is more authentic in its description of the truth than what the witnesses affirm. But there are no witnesses to the happenings of the origins. By their very nature, the ancient texts are witnesses to an extremely advanced stage of the process of what has happened, above all if we remember the millions of years during which the dinosaurs, who left nothing written, dominated the earth! And there is no reason at all to think that our understanding, because it is slightly later than those texts, is more limited than that of our ancestors.

But here, indeed, something rather interesting happens. The ancient accounts of creation are normally accounts of a certain sort of salvation. That is to say, they describe how things came to be what they are now, and this takes the form of describing how the current order of things was installed. Normally they begin with a battle among the gods, and starting from the victory of one of the gods, the earth is established. The victory, it should be said, normally takes the form of a murder, a lynching or a dismemberment. And starting from this, the created order comes into being. This can be seen in particularly luminous form in the epic of Gilgamesh, with the death of Tiamat, but also, for example, in the Rig Veda (10.90) where the dismemberment of a man and the distribution of his members is the creation both of what is and of the Hindu social order.

None of this should surprise us. The only thing that it means is that the answer to the question 'Where do we come from?' is narrated from within the schemes of power and social order which are in force. And the answer tends to maintain and shore up this order. That is why creation is described as a victory over chaos. That is to say, the description of the orgins comes from an understanding of social 'salvation' which was already in evidence within the group in question. The description of what things 'are' is strictly dependent on what they now 'ought' to be.

Well, I would like to suggest that the Jewish notion of creation, on which we are dependent, introduces some notable ruptures within this scheme. If I understand it aright, what we see in the case of the Jewish tradition is what I would call an anti-idolatry movement which only at a very late stage starts to ask itself about the question of creation. As I understand it, the accounts of the origins at the beginning of Genesis are much later than a significant number of the stories in the same book, for example, those of Abraham. And according to the experts, these accounts are from the period of the exile or its aftermath, containing many elements which are critical allusions to Babylonian myths of origin. For example, there is the garden where not the king and the nobles, but merely man and woman have their dwelling. Or indeed the insistence that the first thing created is light, which means that the whole of creation will be luminous, in itself a demythifying move and, keeping things in their due proportion, a secularising one. At the same time it has been noted that the account of creation, although luminous and limpid in comparison with the murders and bloodletting which appear in the Babylonian texts, is

still not entirely free from the notion of creation as the establishment of order in the midst of chaos. That is to say, the famous
'*tohu wa bohu*' of Genesis 1:2 suggests a 'something' out of which
God organised things, and it could be that it contains traces of a
reference to the killing of a sea monster. And starting from that
slain monster everything was created.[1]

However, there is no doubt that we are in the presence of an
anti-idolatry movement which aims at the un-throning of the gods
and all their various and complicated relationships with the social
order, heading for there being one God. In just the same way as
God cannot be involved in a slaughter among the gods, so also God
has to be related to everything that *is* in a different way. And it
seems as though it was the exile, and because of it the loss of real
power over the social order which Yahweh had seemed to have
while he was linked to a monarchy and a Temple, which led to
the new perception: the perception that if we are talking about
God, affirming that God is not among the gods, then there must
be a radical separation between God and the order and establishment of this world. That is to say, one part of an anti-idolatrous
movement is that it is, and has to be, a self-critical movement
concerning the way in which the perception of God is tied to the
social world. Now, it is very easy to say that. But I know very
well from my own experience that going through the experience
of losing the bond between God and the customary order without
losing the notion of God and falling into just one more reaction is
an immensely slow, painful and unpredictable experience. Be that
as it may, it was the impossibility of keeping alive the belief in
God as one of the gods, through their defeat, that led the Jewish
interpreters to one of two alternatives: either Yahweh is a minor
deity who has lost out to more powerful neighbouring deities, or
Yahweh is on a totally different level from the gods, not even
being comparable with them. And that means that any account
which is given of the relationship between God and all that is will
be markedly different.

If this was already visible in the book of Genesis, how much

---

1 There are also hints of this in, for instance, Psalm 89:10.

more is it not visible in Second Isaiah! This book, and above all its chapters 45—48 which were probably written not so many years distant from the accounts of the origins in Genesis, is of a phenomenal exuberance. On reading it I have the impression of being in the presence of texts which are eyewitness descriptions of an extraordinary discovery which had not been understood before, and which now allows more sense to be made of everything. And indeed they are texts of an extraordinary discovery, since they mark the definitive move from monolatry to pure monotheism, and at the same time to an absolutely clean description of creation. Now what I would like to point out is that these two discoveries – that of the oneness of God and that of the cleanness, limpidity of creation – go together and imply each other. Let us take for example Isaiah 45:18–19:

> For thus says the LORD who created the heavens (he is God!), who formed the earth and made it (he established it; he did not create it a chaos, he formed it to be inhabited!): "I am the LORD, and there is no other. I did not speak in secret, in a land of darkness; I did not say to the offspring of Jacob, 'Seek me in chaos.' I the LORD speak the truth, I declare what is right."

The oneness of God has as an immediate consequence that there were no secret deals, bloodlettings, or a chaos, prior to creation, but that God formed the earth in order to be inhabited. That is to say, the relationship between God and everything that is is clean, not hidden, and has a benevolent purpose. And all of this is independent of social order and power.

A further step in this process we see only in the second book of Maccabees (7:28–9) where the mother of seven sons implores a son of hers to accept death rather than break the Law in the following terms:

> "I beseech you, my child, to look at the heaven and the earth and see everything that is in them, and recognize that God did not make them out of things that existed. Thus also mankind comes into being. Do not fear this butcher, but prove worthy

of your brothers. Accept death, so that in God's mercy I may get you back again with your brothers.''

Now what it is interesting to underline here is the fact that, in the space of a couple of verses, two things go together: creation, now indeed conceived for the first time as something out of nothing – *ex nihilo* – and belief in the resurrection. I would like to point out that it is a question not of two different doctrines, but of two implications of the single discovery that God has nothing to do with the current social order, which includes of course the way that that social order is inflected by death. That is to say, here we see that the discovery of creation *ex nihilo* and the discovery of the resurrection are the same discovery, and form part of the discovery that God is so alive and exuberant that he has nothing to do with death or the social order, and that his creative energy has other purposes, such that it is a light matter to die rather than to cross those purposes.

Well, this whirlwind tour through some ancient texts concerning creation has as its purpose to reinforce the impression which I want to get over to you: that we are dealing with a process, and a process where what is being discovered is a very peculiar account of the relationship between everything that is and God. And this discovery was made in the midst of an anti-idolatry movement in the degree to which a whole series of radical separations came to be made, principally the separation between God and the order of this world, and that between God and death. These discoveries were made in the midst of defeat and persecution and are thus organically linked to the growing understanding that God has nothing to do with human violence.

the Christian doctrine of creation is a definitive refinement of this process and must be considered within it

What I would like to emphasise now is that when we talk about creation we are talking about a process of discovering the relationship between everything that is and God, a discovery which is always contemporary, and which has immediate consequences for the perception of the world which surrounds us. Among these consequences is the necessary desacralisation of all that is around us, so that we find ourselves empowered to resist bowing before its supposed forces, empowered, in fact, to live as if those forces did not exist. That is to say, part of the process of the discovery of creation is the discovery of an astonishing freedom with respect to what *is*, since what is seen and perceived, and what *is* are different things. When we see and perceive, we do so still partially from within a world formed by our systems of order, of security, of identity, guaranteed in the last resort by death. And what *is* is not strictly attainable from within a mentality formed in this way. However, in the degree to which we cease to have our mind and heart formed by death, we cease having our mind formed by the perception that the social 'other' which surrounds us and precedes us is hostile, ambivalent, capricious and two-faced, and before which we have to behave dishonestly so as to survive, alleging that we just have to be that way, because things just are that way. This forms part of the discovery that the 'other' which surrounds us and precedes us, is at a totally different level from the customary social 'other': benevolent, limpid, without ambivalence and without ambiguity. That is to say, the relationship between God and everything that is, is gratuitous and trustworthy. And if it is to be trusted, then we need not fear discovering the truth about what is, however little convenient that might seem in its social repercussions.

Now it seems that this is the position of those who believe in Christ. The discovery which was handed on to us by the apostolic witnesses is the definitive discovery, so to speak, of the resurrection, not merely as a final sorting out of accounts, which is to say, as part of a moralistic vision of things, but of something that is present, and able to be lived in the here and now. Thus we can understand something of the refinement which Jesus introduced into the perception of the creation.

If I've understood this aright, what the apostolic group perceived is that when Jesus rose from the dead he revealed in a humanly accessible form not only that God has nothing to do with death, thus putting into question all sacred mechanisms of protection by the expulsion of victims. He revealed more than that. He revealed that the giving of himself to our mechanism of death had been the way in which the Creator himself, who knows not death, has wanted us to form part of creation. That is to say, the relation between God and what *is* took on a clearer and previously unimagined form. The relation is one of a deliberate love which includes us in, and which takes the form of participating with us in the experience of being created so that we might participate with him in the divine life, by being created. This means that the Creator himself wanted to undo the knots of futility in which we found ourselves bound, undo them from within, and, starting from his acting out in our midst, empower us to be personally involved in discovering and bringing into being what is.

Thus do I understand the undeniable fact that the apostolic group understood Jesus as in some way involved in bringing creation to its resplendence. For this reason they speak of Jesus as the one through whom all things were created. In a vision tied to the substitutionary theory of the atonement, Jesus is imagined as (in some way) present 'in the beginning', and then, various millennia later, having got into the bath whose taps he had (in some way) helped to turn on earlier. But in the vision which I am trying to recover, we see creation as forever contemporary in a human activity in our midst precisely in the overcoming of problems which are of a cultural, not a biological nature. That is to say, it is by humanly detoxifying death that Jesus opens for us, who did not know it, not only the true sense of creation, but also the capacity to come to be created children of God by putting into practice ourselves the same overcoming of our culture shot through by death, trusting in a generosity which does not know death, and which will take care of us. Thus do the Scriptures say of him that he is the first born of all creation (Col. 1:15) and at the same time the author and perfecter of faith (Heb. 12:2).

by the gift of the Holy Spirit the Creator himself participates humanly with us in the process of discovering what it is to bring creation to its fullness

Here I would like to make a brief observation concerning the meaning of the gift of the Holy Spirit. If we read the famous chapters 14—16 of John's Gospel, something will be noted which is very similar to the account which I am proposing to you. We see God himself, as a human being, giving his creating Spirit to human beings as a consequence of his going to death so that we be led into all truth. That is to say, the role of the counsel for the defence, the Paraclete, and the role of opener up of all truth by means of the overcoming of victimary processes, and the role of making us participants in bringing creation into being on the same level as Jesus, are the same role. And I notice something here which leaves me astounded. In the model of creation as something fitting into the substitutionary theory of salvation there is a moment when we have to step outside the process of learning, in order to lay hold of a 'divine' viewpoint – that is to say, make a mental leap outside the process so as to be able to 'impose' the supposed divine vision on what surrounds us. However, here the matter is very different. In the model which I am sketching out, and which I hope is in harmony with the Johannine witness, we don't get to receive the divine 'eye' or 'insight', so as to speak, by an intellectual leap outside the human process of discovery. Rather it is from within the process of the forgiving overcoming of group violence that we are carried to discovering all truth. Which is to say, that through the gift of the Holy Spirit we get to participate actively as conscious and knowing beings within God's own creative act.

there is an objective element in our understanding of creation

If everything said so far is on the right track, that is, if it is death and not in the first place sin which is the problem, and salvation is the culmination of the process by which the Saviour empowers us to live as if death were not, confident that death is only the circumscription which is proper to being created contingently, and that being created contingently with our participation will last for ever thanks to the goodness of the One whose project it is; if all this is true, then there is an objective element which follows on as a consequence of the doctrine of creation. But it is not an affirmation concerning a knowledge of our orgins which is supposedly epistemologically independent. It is rather an affirmation with respect to the relation between everything that is and God, in such a way that it allows us to know that our access to what really is, and because of that, our living in reality, opens up for us in the degree to which we overcome the violence of our relationships among ourselves. That is to say: the access to what really is consists, in all our cases, in an access which we reach collectively in the degree in which we do not live according to the gods, but rather from the forgiving victim. Or, said in another way: forgiveness is our access to creation. And I'm not saying this only in some 'religious' or mystical way, but in a sense which has anthropological and sociological consequences. To put this synthetically: in the degree in which we move on from relationships of violence among ourselves, and relationships whose violence is guaranteed 'sacredly', in that degree we come to be able to understand what is and to find ourselves within it.

I'll give some all too obvious examples. Some scientific or intellectual research just cannot be carried out while it implies going against sacred structures, which might well be those of a church, or those of a group of imams, or those of the officials of some government ministry. While things are that way, we never come to understand what is, but rather remain trapped in futility. For truth doesn't get to be discovered except in the degree to which someone doesn't fear reprisals. This freedom from fear comes either because the social group has already learned not to be frightened of the consequences of new discoveries which apparently cause a great shake-up. Or because the researcher doesn't fear death, and believes in the underlying goodness of what they are in the process of discovering, and so are ready to run the risk of going ahead, suffering the consequences, because they desire the good of those who for the moment don't understand, but who in the long run will benefit from the discovery of the truth, difficult though it be to believe so now, to judge by their attitudes. In other words, I am talking about the anthropological conditions of possibility which allow the development of science, of knowledge.

What is key here is that the discovery of the truth about what *is* depends absolutely on a social interaction that is in the process of overcoming a collective delusion. Which is to say, it is forgiveness and the forgiving mentality which is capable of acceding to the truth, because it is the forgiving mentality which is ready to put up with attacks, marginalisation, time-wasting and loss of reputation, leaving these things behind as things of little import, so as to be able to make the truth to shine, truth understood as something for the benefit of all, including those who currently want to know nothing about it.

And there is progress in this in the degree to which we manage to desacralise our world, so as to understand its underlying goodness and trustability; and this not only with relation to the 'gods' of primitive religions, but in the midst of the 'gods' with a partially secular face which throb in our world and which help configure our violent relationships. That is to say, the consequence of the discovery of creation is increasing human responsibility for everything that is, including our way of managing our social relationships which allow us to be related to what is, and without which there is no access to anything. And this growing human responsibility is not the consequence of some 'disenchantment' of the world, or of God's having withdrawn to the margins, but the very exact consequence of the fact that God himself has given us the key to discover and inhabit with God the ordinary and good 'secularity' of everything that is.

The objective dimension of the relationship between salvation and creation turns out to be the fact that the form which salvation takes is the opening out for us of the possibility of participating with ever greater freedom in creation, and that it was an astounding act on the part of God himself to have given us the confidence to be able to do this. This giving us confidence was the revealing of all the dimensions of God's benevolent project through the life, death and resurrrection of Jesus. If Jesus was not a god who was inaugurating a salvation cult by means of a sacrificial trick, very much in the mode of the gods, but God himself, Creator of all things, then salvation is not independent of the necessary opening up of doors towards the bringing creation to its fullness.

from these considerations a beneficent understanding of natural law is born

Shortly before Easter 2002, the Holy Father, in an allocution to the members of the Pontifical Academy for Life, called on Catholic philosophers and scientists to formulate better arguments in favour of natural law, above all in the field of bioethics. In response to this I would like to make a small contribution by underlining some of the consequences of what I am discovering about creation. What I would like to say is the following: that natural law is in the first place an indispensable element of the Christian doctrine of creation precisely because it is the indispensable link between creation and salvation. That is to say, it is our way of insisting that there is not an absolute rupture between that which we see here and now and that which is the divine plan for the fullness of creation. What is now, and what will be, have an organic relationship between themselves, and in principle we can learn from what is now something about its definitive plenitude. In other words, there is a trustable continuity between that which is in need of salvation and that which will appear once saved. This is the consequent way of saying that any attempt to speak about salvation as if it were the abolition of something disastrous and the inauguration of something totally new does not keep alive the necessary unity between our Creator and our Saviour. For that reason, one of the firmest consequences of the insistence on natural law is the denial of the arbitrary or capricious nature of divine commandments. This is evident traditionally in the rejection of the voluntarist and nominalist positions with respect to morals. If God forbids us something it is because doing it does us no good. Which is to say, the holiness of the commandment is in the fact that it is for our good, and it

is not the case that our good is to be found in following commandments independently of their consequences for us, just because
they are commandments.

Well then, if this is valid, we can see that natural law is, in the
first place, and before any of its possibly polemical use in the world
of non-believers, a very powerful instrument of self-criticism with
respect to our own moral teaching. If it is used correctly, the first
consequence of the use of this instrument would be having confidence that we can change our own understanding of morality in
the light of our growing appreciation of what is. And this appreciation of what is grows precisely in the degree to which we learn
not to base our moral teaching on the inherited opinions of our
group with respect to what is 'good' and what is 'bad', but rather
to overcome the tendency to cast out the weak whose existence
is inconvenient to us, and thus to find ourself discovering what
really is. That is to say; leaving behind a world made in the image
and likeness of our group, which closes us into sacred certainties,
so as to discover what *is*, is something different from what we
imagined, and for that reason we have to undergo the restructuring
of our group. To put it another way: natural law would thus be a
very powerful bulwark against the group tendency to constitute
itself into the ghetto of the saved, making of its beliefs something
independent of a process of discovery. In this sense natural law is
the instrument of demythification par excellence. By insisting on
it we keep alive the possibility of being a universal Church, and
by losing it we begin to make of ourselves an exclusive sect.

Now please notice that this is a two-edged sword. On the one
hand it can serve as a critical instrument with relation to practices
which are socially and economically 'convenient' with respect to
the weak and the vulnerable, in the case of abortion, euthanasia,
the rights of immigrants, of racial minorities and so on. That is to
say, it allows the discovery of values which will in fact change
the composition of the group which has a tendency to reject the
possibility that such vulnerable people should be an intrinsic and
constitutive part of it. On the other hand it serves as an internal
critique of ecclesiastical doctrines which start from aprioristic principles and which do not correspond to the discovery of what is,

but rather refuse to participate in that discovery, like for instance the critique, made by the sixteenth-century Spaniards who defended the Indians, of the intellectual structure which allowed the inhabitants of the New World to be treated as slaves; or, closer to home, of the current teaching of the Vatican congregations with relation to gay people.

In any case, I am seeking to demonstrate that within the relationship between salvation and creation which I have been sketching out, there lies the possibility of an understanding of natural law which is much less open to the real criticism which is made of it. The criticism is that it is a subtle a priori defence of doctrinal positions which are never submitted to the possibility that in the light of what is discovered as the world is progressively demystified, these same doctrinal positions might be revealed to be the enemies of the very natural law which they espouse, by being sacred bulwarks erected against enemies, which are necessary to a certain group self-understanding.

Natural law will convince much more when it is not an instrument of ecclesiastical battle, but a process of self-critical discovery, which brings into the light consequences for all, believers and non-believers at the same time.

all this has consequences for how we see ourselves

If everything which I have said so far is true, then it is worthwhile emphasising a consequence in that objective part of our life which is our subjectivity. It means that there is no need to stress ourselves about feeling something 'more' about ourselves when we say that we are created. Understanding ourselves as created is not the application to ourselves of a description deduced from an a priori vision of 'how things came to be', but the growing recognition of ourselves as peripheral recipients on the way towards being brought into existence by a bounteous strength which is massively prior to us, and whose intentions we have no reason to suspect. That is to say, the discovery of the creation towards which we are on the way to being saved reaches us as a profound relaxation and peace. Not the relaxation and peace of those who need to rest, but the relaxation and peace which come together with the sensation of being vivified, quickened, in the degree to which we discover ourselves welcome participants in a stupendous adventure of open horizons and of much greater dimensions than we could be accustomed to think.

conclusion

I hope that it is now possible to see where we have been going in this 'salvation' triptych. I have been attempting to encourage a shift in perception whereby we leave behind a 'theory' which we 'know' and 'hold fast to', as a necessary condition for being on the inside of the group of the saved, who are being saved 'from' the world. I think that that account of salvation sets us up to turn Christianity into a form of ineffectual moral bullying. Instead, I have been trying to give hints of what it might look like to see salvation as a process of induction, opened up for us by Jesus' giving himself into death at our hands, and leading to our finding ourselves empowered to be on the inside of God's creative act. And the meaning and the sense of this creative act are always opening up before us. It is my hope that such a shift in perception will help us develop a fuller and richer sense of the life of worship, prayer, preaching, and the building of community than the impoverished notions to which we have become accustomed. For fruit of this latter sort is the only real test.

confessions of a former marginaholic

I want to cast a sceptical eye at one of the most common forms of discourse which abounds in religious circles and indeed in circles which would probably be horrified to be thought of as religious. This is a way of talking about, and from, the experience of alienation and marginalisation in which these experiences are taken to be something particularly sacred or holy. I am going to do this by attempting to question some of my own experiences 'out loud'. My experience, or rather my attempted temporary enfolding into discourse of a number of different experiences, is that in my case at least, talk of marginalisation and alienation has often enough been an excuse to talk bunk, and pernicious bunk at that.

I am not making this claim as someone who has always been above such things, or who has not indeed been strongly driven by the considerable moral force which goes along with the thought patterns and feelings which kick in when talk turns to marginalisation, estrangement, alienation and so on. *Au contraire*. It has been a considerable part of my lot and portion over the last twenty years or so to have danced more or less feverishly to these tunes. My claim is that of the recovering marginaholic.

Let me try and fill in what I mean. Some fifteen years ago I went to live in Brazil to do my theological studies. It was the height of the boom in liberation theology, and my way of dealing with my own sense of marginalisation as a gay man who was unable to fit in with any of the recognised power structures in my country, that is to say, to belong to anything at all, was to get out of my country, to go into exile. It is, after all, much easier to be

a non-belonger in a country which is not yours than to find yourself not belonging in what is your own country. Once in Brazil, I
tried to face the world of AIDS which had, at that time, begun to
emerge with ever greater force in that country. As a gay man with
a conscience still bound by the voices of society and Church, AIDS
was my link in to the possibility of being good, the ground on
which I would justify myself, prove that I might after all be a
'good thing'.

One of the things I remember with a certain pleasure at that
time was when one of the leading voices of liberation in my community solemnly informed me that working with people with
AIDS wasn't really a liberating thing at all, since it didn't transform society. The only way to transform society was to work with
a political party or a trades union. This of course merely confirmed
me in what I had begun to suspect about the liberation 'thing',
which is that its doyens had a peculiar knack of associating liberation with things which wouldn't cause them to lose their
reputations. And thus I was able to be even more marginalised
than the self-appointed guardians of holy marginalisation. Which
means, of course, even more holy. My sense of who I was was
very much dependent on being rejected, since I knew, or thought
I knew, that that was what the Gospel demanded, and I had
managed to fool myself that my search for being marginalised was
of God.

How did this pan out in the actual time I spent with people
dying from AIDS? I have not yet been able to give any satisfactory
account to myself of this time spent, and what it means. I hope
that the people I accompanied will welcome me into the heavenly
halls as their brother. But if so, then it will be because they have
been able to see through the mixed motives and hugely complex
series of needs which I brought to what I was vaguely aware, even
then, had more to do with me than with them. Let me put it this
way: it was as though I was a voyeur of those who occupied the
place of shame and ultimate marginalisation, knowing that I was
terrified of being where they were, not only because of the disease
and its ravages, but because of the shame involved. As a priest I
was able, of course, to offer them sacraments and the other gifts

of priestly ministry, and I remember even then being struck by how they were able to receive a power and transforming grace from the sacraments, a power and grace which had absolutely nothing to do with my subjectivity, whose eyes were scarcely daring to look at what I was doing. It was as if in fact the sign was working quite independently of its minister, who was a sort of Baalam's ass of *ex opere operato* grace.

Looking back now, I think I can see what was missing in this powerful compulsion to such ambiguous compassion. And I will try to develop that in a little. In a nutshell, however, what was missing was the ability to like anyone. Either them, or myself. It was though I was dancing terrified before the veil of a ghastly reality which I didn't dare to go through, while unable to like either those on this side or those on that side of the veil.

Something of this became even clearer to me when I moved, later, to Bolivia. You can't, I thought to myself, get much more marginalised than living in Bolivia; surely therefore it must be an heroically holy thing to choose to work here. And yet one of my abiding memories of the eighteen months I spent in that beautiful, and indeed severely marginalised, country, at whose Catholic university I taught, was of my complete inability to like the place or its people. Yet again I managed to inspire others to find it necessary to get rid of me, and yet again I set myself up to become holy by being rejected – what I have referred to in a book I wrote as 'the self-canonization of the self-victim'.[1]

It was as though I was not dealing with a real place and real people, but with some sort of sounding board which I needed at which to hurl my own white, gay, middle-class etc. etc. angst. Though here too, and maybe a little more clearly, not far beneath the surface of my own apparently confident self-presentation there were gnawing doubts as to whether I wasn't really engaged in something that was far from holy: wandering around, as a friend of mine pointed out, after I had managed to figure for the nth time at the centre of a bout of sacrificial violence, with a large label pinned to my back saying 'Kick me.'

---

1. *Raising Abel* (New York: Crossroad, 1996), p. 184.

I guess the breakthrough happened in the period following this, when three things came together over the course of a year: first, I managed to finish my doctoral thesis, thus finishing off for the first time an educational process and feeling for the first time in my life that I had successfully completed something; second, the Dominican superiors in South America joined forces to get rid of me (something for which, I should make quite clear, I am, at this stage, profoundly grateful); and third, the man I loved in Brazil died suddenly and unexpectedly three weeks into his first opportunistic infection after some ten years of being HIV+ (this was all before the cocktail of drugs currently in use became available).

In retrospect, these three events set off a process which I can only refer to as dying, such that a couple of years after them I began to understand that I had died. Let me try to explain. My doctoral thesis (appropriately called 'The Joy of Being Wrong'[2]) had been, for some time, my way of surviving, holding on to doing something worthwhile, and to achieving something. About six months before I finished, a French Dominican asked me what was my ambition in life, and I said: to finish my thesis. The truth was that I didn't have any ambitions after that, because I just wanted to die, but needed to have done at least something first, and this, I hoped, would be it.

However, the truth was that, as I finished my thesis, I began to realise that I was now ready to go, since I simply didn't have any ambition, any desire to do anything left. Heroically finishing a thesis in the midst of persecution was it, and when desire ran out, there was nothing but dying left to do. There was also a strange sense, as I finished the thesis, that I had somehow been reached by whatever is meant by 'there is now no condemnation for those who are in Christ'.[3] And this was accompanied by a certain interior collapsing with relief. Some sort of battle was over. Having no ambition left, and nothing to win, and faced only with a desire to

2. Later published under that same title (New York: Crossroad, 1998).
3. Rom. 8:1.

die, maybe I was in a position to begin to be empowered to 'walk not after the flesh but after the spirit'.[4]

Then there was the repudiation by the Dominican superiors in South America, experienced by me both as a clean break, and thus a relief, and of course as a shock. What I perceived them as saying to me was 'Your attempt to have a life project here in this continent has failed, it is over. You are not one of us.' And they were, of course, quite right. I had obscurely been using them as I had been using those I had accompanied with AIDS, and as I had been using the idea of Bolivia. They even had the decency to repudiate me in such a violent and irrational way that I was spared the humiliation of having to recognise publicly that they were right, and that I had been barking up the wrong tree for years. I was able to go off with my dignity of the 'destroyed one' intact, so bad did they make themselves look. But at the same time, I knew, deep down, and rejoiced that I had been let off, my membership of the religious order annulled, and I was deeply relieved that the game was up. I was, I should say, also simply terrified of what this would mean: I had no idea of any other way of living than the institutionally protected way in which I had been bound up all my life, and the idea of making a living, surviving off my own bat, was completely terrifying to me. So it did take something like a year before I dared, with my hands covering my eyes, to walk the plank and fall into the rest of my life. But this experience was also a form of death: the death of a whole fake life project and all the props for survival which it afforded: home, country, 'family', profession, training, ability to be of worth in public, ability to tell a life story which makes sense. These are things usually lost at death.

Then the third element of my dying was the death of my friend Laércio in Brazil (I was in Chile at the time, packing my stuff so as to go back and be with him, since at that time 80 per cent of seropositive patients died within five months of presenting their first symptom). Again, in retrospect, what happened here was that at last, and for the first time, I had actually managed to make a

---

4. Rom. 8:4.

decision on my own to do something genuinely loving: to go back and be with someone, however precariously that involved living; and I was caught unawares while moving ahead. My last ambition had died and I had literally nothing left to do. But there was much more than that. In the days after his death I realised that the love was genuine, nothing to be ashamed of, and that it was possible, and this was actually what life was all about, a completely new and destabilising possibility in the light of which my careful protection against life while dancing on the edge of marginality was completely disarmed. I knew this as a sense of not really having lost him at all, and even as a sense that the only way I could respond in gratitude and thus in gratuity to him was actually to accept this kick into life which he was offering me.

Furthermore, something else gradually dawned on me: since I found myself actually loving him, I also found that the place of shame which had been made visible for me by the presence of gay men dying of AIDS was suddenly no longer a place of shame. If Laércio, whom I loved, and knew to be wonderful, could have undergone this place of shame and death, then so could I. It didn't hold any terror for me any longer, or any fascination. I was no longer dancing frenziedly round the edge of the veil, but had found myself sucked through it. Simultaneously with this there was the sense of having at last been able to grasp something of what Jesus' promise of eternal life was about, and of baptism as undergoing death in advance, so as no longer needing to live with death as something in the foreground. It is not as though shame were suddenly cancelled; rather I discovered that shame held in love as something tender and delicate is not really shame at all, but a certain rejoicing.

These then were the three factors which seemed to combine in my experience of dying: loss of ambition and the need to succeed, loss of a fake and compulsive life project, and transformation of a defining shame into something which holds neither fear nor fascination, and with it the possibility of just being, and liking being, human.

Well, in the light of this, if light it be, I would like to try and talk about life in the place where death is somehow behind me.

And the sense I have is that what is growing on me is the notion of being an heir, of receiving an inheritance.

Let me explain. The passage I have in mind is this:

> If you are Christ's, then you are Abraham's offspring, heirs according to promise. I mean that the heir, as long as he is a child, is no better than a slave, though he is the owner of all the estate; but he is under guardians and trustees until the date set by the father. So with us; when we were children, we were slaves to the elemental spirits of the universe. But when the time had fully come, God sent forth his Son, born of woman, born under the law, to redeem those who were under the law, so that we might receive adoption as sons [and daughters]. And because you are sons [and daughters], God has sent the Spirit of his Son into our hearts, crying, "Abba! Father!" So through God you are no longer a slave but a son [or daughter], and if a son [or daughter] then an heir. Formerly, when you did not know God, you were in bondage to beings that by nature are no gods; but now that you have come to know God, or rather to be known by God, how can you turn back again to the weak and beggarly elemental spirits, whose slaves you want to be once more? (Gal. 3:29—4:9)

Now I guess what I want to say is this. The heir is the owner of the estate. There is absolutely nothing marginal at all about being the owner of the estate. In fact, it is difficult to imagine anything more central than being the owner of the estate. It's all going to come to you. Whatever is going on, and whatever battles and squabbles and so forth seem to be running the show, whoever seems to be in and whoever's out, it doesn't matter one bit to you, because you're the heir, and you're going to inherit it all, anyhow.

And this corresponds to my experience of living as having died, which I attempted to describe to you earlier. That is to say, I seem to find a growing sense of being in on the centre of what it's all about. And this is not a counterfactual claim to power, because it is not a claim at all. Rather it is a discovery of being given something which is also a being given to be someone exactly in the degree to which I am taking part in a huge, and largely hidden adventure.

I want to try to tease out several dimensions of this experience of receiving an inheritance, since I am not quite sure where it's all going. The first dimension is that of being in on the centre of things without being the centre. It is Christ who is in the centre of the experience, the one who occupies the place of shame and marginalisation and victimage. And because he occupies it freely, and because he likes us, it means that there is a strange sense both of being in on the centre, because he has made it a place not to be feared, and yet, because it is no longer a sacred space, and thus a frightening space, of there being no centre at all any more, and thus the centre being everywhere, including where I am. A bit like an existential version of Pascal's description of God as a circle whose centre is everywhere and whose circumference is nowhere.[5]

This for me finds concrete form in a sense of the eucharistic Christ both collapsing the Temple and the 'Church' in as far as these are institutions with sacred centres of mimetic fascination, and at the same time actively creating a new temple, or founding the Church, as something which is universal since it has no centre and thus no periphery. Being an heir means, or appears to me to mean, finding myself in on that collapse and in on that new creation as a receptive participant. It's my project, and yet it is my project as not mine at all, but given to me to be part of.

I guess that one of the side effects of this growing sense is that of not being able to take terribly seriously the need both to be 'for' the Church and 'against' it, which seems to be so strong with us. Rather as though our goodness depends on there being a Church, but also we need to kick against it in order to be good – that's a certain sort of occupying the centre and the margins at the same time, but it now seems to me that it's the sort of occupation of centre and margins which is riven with a need to justify oneself over against some other, for there to be bad guys by bat-

---

5. *Pensées* n. 72, though the saying is much older and said to have been traced to a lost treatise of Empedocles (see *Oxford Dictionary of Quotations* [fourth edition], p. 16, no. 17).

tling with whom I become good. In short, it seems to me the sort of addictive pattern of desire that is tied up with not being able to receive death and goodness and life as gifts to be relaxed into so as not to have to hold on to anything at all. It is rather extra-ordinary to find myself not being ashamed of being an insider, or of being an outsider, because there is no longer an inside and an outside.

A second dimension of the experience of receiving an inheri-tance is, in apparent contradiction with the point about non-sacred centrality, a sense of being on the periphery. And I use periphery rather than margins deliberately. This is the sense that there is such an overwhelming power and presence of the centre, linked with Christ and God's dynamic movement towards us so as to involve us as active shared participants in creation, that it is delightful to be a relatively irrelevant peripheral recipient of all this goodness. If I can make a bit more sense of this, it is the perception that the 'other' which, as René Girard has taught me,[6] is always massively prior to the formation of an 'I' or a 'self', is also hugely and powerfully benevolent, and that it is OK to relax into receiving and being swept up by this power and this benevol-ence, to let go.

However, as I said, this sense of being peripheral to a hugely benevolent powerful other is not the same as being 'marginal' at all. Since it includes the realisation that there is no one who is not just such a peripheral; and there is the possibility of being able to discover fellow peripherals, to whom I am able to relate as ones undergoing the same reception of inheritance and being called into rejoicing. But with a difference. None of us has to achieve any-thing, to get anything right, to be a success, and therefore it becomes possible to rejoice in others with whom I am in no sort of competition, and thus I do not need to protect myself against their mortality, their time-wasting, their deficiencies, or mine,

---

6. See, for instance, *Resurrection from the Underground: Feodor Dostoevsky* (New York: Crossroad, 1997); or *I See Satan Fall like Lightning* (New York: Orbis Books/Leominster: Gracewing, 2001).

because it is as such that we are liked and are being given to be something new.

Sacred centres produce margins, and the margin is a dangerous place to be, and much effort must be expended not to be among the losers, whether in terms of finance, health, reputation or whatever. However, the extraordinarily powerful, benevolent, non-sacred, non-centre, which is Christ building the new Temple, is able to make it a pleasure to dwell with spaciousness among the weak and those of little account, because there is, after all, 'world enough and time'. So peripheral existence enables liking being among those who do not have anywhere to go, because they are neither competition, nor sign of scarcity, not threat of loss, nor object of compassion, but sign of gift and shared story. There is all the spaciousness of eternal life with which to begin to build a story of the sort that has no end.

My third dimension for teasing out is that of complacency. Isn't there something complacent about this sense of receiving an inheritance which is the opposite of all those rather athletic-sounding New Testament exhortations about striving, and persevering and so on? At least there are little voices from my old self kicking in to tell me that I should, like a good evangelical, be doing more about things. But I think those voices are wrong. The first point about complacency is that, contrary to its bad name, it is in fact rather a good thing, because it means dwelling with liking in something. The Father says of his Son, 'This is my son in whom I am complacent.' If you want to know that I am not making this up, here's St Jerome's translation: *'Tu es Filius meus dilectus in te conplacui.'*[7] If the Father dwells with liking in or on someone, then to like being liked, to go along with that being liked, strange though it may seem, is surely a rather important part of receiving the regard of the Father. It is only presumption if it is held on to as something which is no longer being received, but as already held, and is thus something independent of further delighted growth into the regard of the one who takes pleasure. We tend to use complacency only in the sense of a closed-off being-pleased-

7. Mark 1:11 (Vulgate).

with-oneself which cuts one off from further involvement with or vulnerability towards others.

However, I'd like to suggest, and I think that this is what I am experiencing over time, that just as complacency can shade off into presumption, so it can also, and more properly, deepen into compassion. That is, it is someone who is liked who can appreciate what is really likeable about someone, and bring that out. I remember a story in one of the London free weekly gay papers (*Boyz*, I think) about a man who, together with his boyfriend, rented a porno video. Unbeknown to the man, his boyfriend had previously acted in porno videos of a rather violent and disturbing sort before they met. The shop assistant at the video store that evening put the wrong video into the box, and – hey presto – they suddenly found themselves watching a film in which one of them was starring, if being repeatedly raped for the pleasure of others counts as starring. Needless to say the former actor rushed out of the room with shame and fear at his being uncovered, and only dared to come back in several hours later, where he found his boyfriend just sitting and crying in front of a blank TV screen. The former actor imagined that this meant that it was all over between them and that he should collect his things and move out. But no, it turned out that the boyfriend was crying because of the debasement to which someone he loved had subjected himself, or been subjected; he was crying with compassion as he saw something of the sort of deep dark place his partner must have been in, in order to have got himself into something like that.

I suggest that only someone who is really aware of being liked, who is really complacent, is able to defuse someone else's place of shame and make it spacious. And it is out of complacency that liking flows to those who are like: because I am not frightened of being like someone, liking them, being liked by them. Thus being able to share with them in something as equals becomes not a demand or a burden placed on a tortured will, but part of the discovery of who I am as I find myself being turned into something different by a spacious sharing with someone who I am like.

There is something deeply non-moralistic about this, because it means that we find ourselves learning to receive the other as gift. Now, as will be apparent, I am here extrapolating from hints of something I hope to receive rather than describing something which is my pacific possession! But I think that it does rather turn on its head the sting of the question of marginalisation, alienation and estrangement as demand, as burden, as reproach. I've felt that sting often enough, and part of the tension of marginalisation as demand is that relaxation into being loved is felt to be something selfish, something that detracts from the sacrificial giver I ought to be. And I have experienced this as a kind of fear that if I had it good, if I were loved and contented, then I would be insensitive to the marginal other, I would quickly become invulnerable to the demands of the victim.

So there is a sort of trap: I must be discontent and marginalised in order to be attentive to those on the margin, and yet sense that while acting in that way, it may be only my own drama that I am acting out; there may be no real 'other' in my ken. On the other hand, if I discover myself as loved, and start to relax into that regard, or to realise what Paul meant when he said, 'But now that you have come to know God, or rather to be known by God',[8] in that passage I quoted earlier – and I bring to your attention this introduction of the passive verb, with the sense that one has discovered one's being in the being known by God, as the periphery of God's regard. If, as I say, I start to relax into that regard, then will I not in my complacency lose my anguished sensitivity to the other? Will my ears not become dull to the cry of the oppressed, and my eyes blind to the sufferings of the victim, and will I thus not miss out on salvation?

Well, what I see dissolving in this experience of receiving an inheritance, is exactly this sense of a trap. One of the fruits of discovering oneself in the loving regard of God is an ability to like and be liked, and thus to be curious and unthreatening and experimental and creative in relationship to others, but also to trust that I will be given both the things needed to assure me of

---

8. Gal. 4:9. A reading of this passage is further developed in Chapter 9 of this book.

being loved, and the irruptions of the other which will keep me vulnerable to gratuity; that I will, in my sense of being loved, become more sensitive to, and awestruck by, the other — the heroism, the achievement, the pain — and not less so. This is not just some sort of consolation to keep me happy. It is because the other who can irrupt in my life and cause me to become someone different, to tell a story embracing elements of being human I couldn't imagine, is other as gift, and it is only as gift that they are other. In fact it is only as gift that the marginal other really is other to me, part of my upbuilding by God, rather than part of my defence of a controlled being and an appropriation of goodness, the necessary sounding board to my own tale of tragic heroism.

I guess that what I am talking about here (and it probably sounds very banal, and it goes back to the root of my shame and batting about the margins) is being given a heart. I was so ashamed that I didn't have a heart, that I didn't have any of the right reactions, didn't feel compassion, pity, love, and was so ashamed that I would be found out as being this heartless person, that I covered up for this by fleeing to the ends of the earth, putting myself in places where because no one would be able to understand me, they wouldn't be able to discern the huge hole where a heart should be.

And what could be a greater inheritance than actually to receive the heart of the One who only knows marginality, alienation and scarcity, pain and death as surds which weigh too heavily on those he would empower creatively to imagine their way into playfulness?

being wrong and telling the truth

It is a very great privilege for me to stand before you, as one of a series of speakers delivering a Millennium Lecture in this parish.[1] That the speakers who have come before me in this series, many of them cardinals and theologians of great reputation and prestige, have been people of much greater authority than I, gives me great relief. This is because I want to do something with you for which I have no authority. And I want to do it, confident that this parish, and those who attend these lectures, are exposed with frequency and in depth to those who speak with authority, and therefore will not be scandalised by what is going to be an exercise in speaking without authority. I am confident that you will be able to separate the wheat from the chaff, or regard everything I say as chaff, as the case may be. Because what I will say this evening I will say on no authority at all other than my own, which is no authority at all. If anything I say is true, then it is the authority of the truth which will impose itself, not the authority of the one speaking.

I have been invited to continue developing in your midst some of the ideas with which I grappled in my recent book *Faith beyond*

---

1. I have decided to maintain the original 'lecture' format of this chapter. It seems to me to be intrinsic to what I have to say that it is the result of a specific invitation to talk in this way by a Catholic parish (St Joseph's in the Village, in New York City, in May 2002). In other words, I was responding to a genuine request for a clarification, rather than pushing a line at an unwilling audience. Furthermore it was a request from a group of people who are perfectly capable of discussing matters of faith without being scandalised, having had a significant number of lectures from highly authorised sources. Such a context is not accidental to any ability I show here to be able to dare to be wrong and to try to tell the truth.

Resentment: Fragments Catholic and Gay. In particular, a member of the parish asked whether I would address the issue of what it means to say that the Church is wrong on the gay issue. I welcome this question very warmly because it gives me a chance to dwell on what I think to be the only really important question around the gay issue in the Church, which is whether the current teaching of the Vatican congregations is true or not. I consider all discussions about gay men in the priesthood and the current wave of scandals to be secondary to this question of truth, though linked to it in a very marked degree. I also welcome the question because it obliges me to stand before you bereft of all clothes but my own. This is because I do not think that the current teaching of the Vatican congregations is true. I am well aware that for a convinced, and somewhat conservative Catholic, for such do I consider myself to be, and such are some of you, to address the issue of whether such current teaching is untrue is to take a step into a very frightening space, the space where I may well be wrong, may be leading my brothers and sisters astray, encouraging them down a dark path of self-deception. I am well aware that to cause scandal to the faithful by leading astray in a matter of doctrine is a terrible thing to have on one's conscience, and of course, as a theologian, my fidelity to my vocation will be judged by whether I have borne witness to the One calling, and made available that One's words to my brothers and sisters, or whether I have, in the splendid words of the Anglican *Book of Common Prayer*, 'followed too much the devices and desires of my own heart', and borne witness only to those devices and those desires.

I only feel able to embark upon this course of suggesting that the current teaching of the Vatican congregations is wrong, for one simple reason, and it is one of the reasons I am overjoyed to be a Catholic, and that is that we are in this together. I am delighted to rest in the certainty that the One who loves us and calls us into communion with him will not allow such a person as the one speaking to you to lead you too far astray without providing the means to lead us into all truth. And I am also sure that if my attempt to say why I think the current teaching is false be conducted with appropriate courtesy and tentativeness, then the

One who makes the truth resplendent will have no difficulty in turning even my falsehoods into paths by which we may be called to live in the truth.

Yet I am also aware that the truth will not shine unless people stand up for it and are prepared to run risks for it. I want therefore to put my credibility on the line by saying: this is what seems to me to be true, and this false, and I suggest that we must live accordingly. I am confident that if what I say is true, then whatever the current reaction within the Church, in the long run it will be found to have its place in the developing of our reception of the Good News brought to us by Jesus Christ. And if not, not.

So let me proceed with what I think to be the most useful and least scandalous way to approach this very delicate subject, which is to set out where I think I'm coming from.

In the first place, I am not in a position to say 'such and such people have got something wrong. I have got something right.' This is for two reasons. The first is that I don't think I've got anything right – rather I think that I'm scrabbling after something which I will never possess alone, only as part of the Church; and the second is my sense that the discussion can only be a useful one if we find ourselves agreeing that it is we, the Church, who have got something wrong. Because we are not dealing with information which some have, and others haven't, but with the workings of the Holy Spirit in the midst of the people of God over time. Over a very long time. So this is my first point. Before we even come to a discussion about Roman teaching, which is a comparatively small matter, what I would like to suggest is that we, the Catholic Church, have got something wrong in our reception of the Good News. It is as a group over time that we have got this something wrong. And like all things which are wrong, its wrongness can be seen in the fruit which it has borne and bears over time.

What I would like to suggest is that this process of discovering ourselves to have got something wrong is actually part of what it means to be a Catholic. If we approach the matter this way, then we can be set free from one of the deep pains which any Catholic goes through as they come to discover that something which seemed to be good and sacred is in fact not good, and not sacred. For it is not as though some wicked people have been duping us on the gay issue, people who knew something we didn't and held us in thrall. If one feels that way about things being got wrong, then it leads one to adopt the position of the innocent dupe over against the wicked conspirator. I read once in a history of the Reformation in Germany of the shame and anger felt by many who had, in good faith, bought indulgences from Tetzel or one of his colleagues, and which, in the light of the preaching of the Reformation, they had discovered to be worthless pieces of paper. They had discovered themselves duped by charlatans, who were operating within a system which seemed to lend a sacred authority to their charlatanry, and whose members no doubt didn't think of themselves as charlatans at all. The experience of those who had bought the indulgences and discovered their worthlessness was one of the loss of being able to be Catholic.

But I am talking about something slightly different. I am talking about discovering *as* Catholics that we have been wrong. Not only those who have taught the Gospel in a way which makes it a stumbling block for gay people, but those who have gone along with it out of fear, those who have gone along with it in good conscience, and those who don't care, but have been happy to go along with it, because it seems to back up the natural order of things. And such, at one time or another, have been most of us.

And here's a further point which derives from this claim of mine that we have got something wrong. Many of us are used to discussions about conscience which seem to suggest that the following is a useful way of proceeding: 'We know what the teaching of the Church is, and we also know that it has a teaching on conscience, and that one should obey one's conscience even when that conflicts with the teaching of the Church.' Well, I am, of course, in a way doing just that this evening, by speaking my mind on something within the Church. But I find myself in deep sympathy with the most conservative theological position on conscience which regards it as something created by and for truth, and only capable of real delight when held in the truth. Sometimes when the issue is treated as one of conscience, then the issue of whether the teaching is true or not gets put on a back-burner. But that is what I want to avoid. What I am suggesting is that we as Church have got something wrong. That we are not receiving the fullness of truth, and that our current teaching is an obstacle to truth rather than a path to it. If someone were to say, against the universal finding of science, 'I think Black people are inferior to Caucasians, and that it is following my conscience to treat them accordingly', we would be very keen that they learn to follow truth rather than their conscience.

No, when I say that we as Church have got something wrong, I am not begging for the space to be allowed to hold a dissident opinion. I don't want to hold a dissident opinion at all. I want to be possessed by the truth, and I think that the Church of which I am part is currently hobbled by an element of untruth, which means we are wrong, and must seek to be accountable to what is, in a way in which we are currently not accountable, and this is not because we must be nice to gay people, or try to get church authority to be nice to gay people, but because I think we are failing to be Catholic by persisting in an error about what is.

I would also like to say that what I am talking about is part of a process of discovery, not a simple deduction. It is not as though I, or anyone else, have worked out from first principles that the Church is wrong. It is rather that in the light of the gradual discovery of what is true, we begin to be able to look at what we have held to be true, and find that it is not true, or at least, not in the form in which it has long been held to be true. In other words, the discovery that something is wrong is the result of a certain shift in understanding brought about by circumstances and forces bigger than ourselves, so that a way of looking at the world and what is in it comes to seem a damaging and dangerous trap which closes down the possibilities of being the sort of beings we are, rather than one which is open-ended towards greater understanding, greater responsibility, greater freedom. In other words, what is true is not something which we can grasp or manipulate. It is something which imposes itself on us over time, and in its light we can confidently say: something is wrong.

So how do we start to say 'The Church has got something

wrong'? In the first place, I reckon by making a distinction between something which is essential to our salvation, and something which is a consequence of our reception of what is essential to our salvation. This is something rather akin to what the Congregation for the Doctrine of the Faith did when, in its document *Ad tuendam fidem*, it made the distinction between different orders of truths. The effort of distinguishing between such teachings as are part of our salvation, and such as are derived from it with greater or lesser degrees of certitude and importance seems to me to be a worthwhile one. Curiously, what I want to say at this point is that when we raise the question of whether the Church has got something wrong in its understanding of the gay question, I don't think that in fact we are dealing with a question of doctrine. Questions of doctrine concern issues such as the oneness and trinitarian relationality of God, the discovery that God became incarnate as the human being Jesus of Nazareth, that his death and resurrection worked our salvation, and that he continues to be present in our midst especially through the sacraments, as part of a loving plan to reconcile us with God by calling us into new being as a new community called Church and enabling us to share God's life for ever.

When we start talking about the gay issue I'm not sure that it is either right or helpful to talk about an error of doctrine. I suspect that it is both more accurate and more useful to talk about an area of mendacity. Because we are not dealing here with an understanding of how God worked our salvation, but of who we are who are being saved. So, I would like to say that what I think we find ourselves inhabiting is an area of mendacity – if you like, a field formed by a dishonesty that is both structural and customary, rather than an area of erroneous doctrine. It is the area of mendacity which has informed our doctrine, and it is the area of mendacity which is now being challenged by new possibilities of finding ourselves accountable to the truth of what is.

I should say that I am not making this move – to challenge an area of mendacity rather than a doctrine – because I think that this will make the task of truth-telling easier, by diminishing the possibility of devastating change which will result from the eventual adjustment of the teaching to what is. It is not merely an attempt to fly beneath the radar of those who feel that they must maintain current teaching as it stands out of fidelity to the Gospel. I have no doubt at all that the change in the life of the Church introduced by the tiniest official recognition that what I, and others like me, are saying might be true will be simply enormous. I think, for instance, that a Catholic Church in which there is no clerical closet would be scarcely recognisable to us, because we are only just beginning to sense quite how much of the current structuring of our Church is dependent on the maintenance of the clerical closet. But I think that the movement towards a communion of people in which there is no closet is of the Gospel, and that not to move towards embracing that discovery, which is already alive and kicking in our midst, is to do deep damage to our chance of being what we are called to be: a universal sacrament of salvation.

No, I am making the distinction between doctrine and what I have called a field of mendacity because I think it corresponds to what we are discovering: an anthropological truth which, I think, has become available to us precisely because of the truth of the Gospel. That is to say, my claim is that in the light of the salvation opened up for us by Jesus Christ, we are immersed in an ongoing process of learning something new about who we are that we didn't know, and that this discovery is learned by us through our discovering ourselves to have been wrong about who we are, and in our consequent treatment of each other and ourselves.

So, to my field of mendacity. I want to make it quite clear that this field of mendacity is and always has been simply part of human culture, rather than something specific to the Church. And that it is here that the Church has an evangelising role to play, both as witness to and part of an inherited field of mendacity, and witness to and part of its overcoming. To put it in a nutshell, what we are discovering about being human is quite simple: that there are certain human beings who, for reasons which are not clear to anyone, are, irrespective of cultural differences, and of social mores, principally attracted at a profound emotional and erotic level to members of their own sex; that this is, in the vast majority of cases, a lifelong attraction, and that such people flourish and are happy when they find themselves able to develop somewhat the same forms of human life as others, principally the ability to tell the truth, and secondarily the ability to relate to others in a straightforward and transparent way, including the possibility of forming lifelong partnerships with others of their free choice. In other words, we are discovering that there are such things as gay people, and that their flourishing happens in exactly the same way, *mutatis mutandis*, as that of everybody else. Which is to say that they are not defective heterosexuals, but just are that way.

Now I want to say that this doesn't sound like rocket science, here in New York in 2002. But it is. This discovery, which is, I would say, quite simply that of a fact about being human, and which therefore affects all humans directly or indirectly, is a discovery which it has taken a long time to make, and is, in its way, just as much an achievement of our race as the discovery of the roundness of our planet, of the heliocentric nature of the planetary system of which we are part and of the human similarity and equality of races other than our own, discoveries which in themselves were bitterly contested in their time, and are now simply taken for granted almost everywhere. It is also similar to the anthropological discovery, rather more important than those others, which is that we can detect our own lies about ourselves when we try to build our unity by scapegoating, because we can recognise an innocent victim. And in fact it is this latter discovery, which is concentric with Christian revelation, which has enabled us to dare to make the other discoveries. I also want to suggest that it is this anthropological discovery very precisely which has enabled us to make our current discovery about the simple and straightforward existence of gay people.

What I want to suggest is that this sort of discovery is only made very gradually, and it is made in the midst not of simple ignorance, but of an area of mendacity which gives the impression of being true, natural, solid and sacred, but is not. And this means that for those within it, and for those coming out of it, the world will look very different indeed. It will in fact be a different world.

Now here is my suggestion: supposing that we accept that there is such a thing as being gay, and that it is simply a fact of life, rather like rain, or tides, or left-handedness, we can then look back at previous cultural life and start to see how mendacity worked in such cultures as have denied this, which means, until very recently, our own. One of the principal ways it worked has been, of course, in some cultures, by giving a special positive status to gay people, such that they were more likely to become the shamans, the magic men, or the priest/prostitutes. This is mendacious, for it ties a quite simple human way of being to a special religious destiny or vocation, and thus helps tie a particular sexual form to the sacred, which can work both ways. Something can be particularly close to the sacred, and particularly abominable to the sacred. In both cases, we are dealing with the world of idols from which Christ came to set us free. A world in which being gay is special is also a world in which it is potentially abominable, and in neither case have we acceded to the equality of fraternity and simple, unremarkable humanity which is what the Gospel offers us as part of an universe free of idols.

Another of the ways in which mendacity has worked in this area is by making it almost impossible to discover that there is such a thing, normally, as being gay, because of the grotesquely distorted relationships between males in general. Ours is a world in which a standard part of male togetherness has included denigrating women, to such a degree that when a group of males conquered another group of males, the way of maximally shaming those others was by raping them, thus reducing them to the status of 'women'. Nothing to do with sex, everything to do with power. And here the military practices of the Ancient Middle East, documented and referred to in our scriptural texts, have had a long history. But exactly the same reality can be seen on a scale never imagined by the most vicious tyrants of old in the modern American penitentiary system, with its effective institutionalisation of male rape.

Not surprisingly, this practice of shaming makes the association of loving relationships between men (and these have traditionally been thought much more threatening than those between women) to be deeply ambivalent, because we are dealing with something which is always teetering on the brink of the shame-filled. And of course, there is little which fosters mendacity, or indeed murder, as much as shame. So we developed a world which depended on male togetherness, and even on male respect and friendship, but which always contained within it the need for some people to hide a shameful truth, that there might be more to such and such a relationship than met the eye. Thus the principal access to dealing with the presence of anomalous people was to codify their behaviour within forms of morality. Ways were found of describing people which can be described as a huge, and very typically masculine, 'Don't ask, don't tell'. Provided you sing the tribal song, and don't get caught, then the proverbial blind eye can be turned to anomalous things you do.

And of course, it is true that the history neither of the West nor of any other part of the world, as far as I know, has been one of unremitting hostility towards gay people. The reality has been far subtler and more nuanced than that. But it has been a reality where definitions could change very quickly, and accepted cultural forms could easily and suddenly be overturned in the face of a threat. As you know, gay people, along with Jews and gypsies, have been the traditional half-insider half-outsiders in most European countries, and at a time of threat it is just such people who are blamed and persecuted.

But, for a complex series of cultural reasons, the male togetherness which has been the staple for most societies most of the time, particularly the militarily successful and expansive ones, has been put in question by the emergence of the demands for a recognition of the full humanity of women. And of course, wherever that has happened, male togetherness has begun to be punctured, to look silly. And of course, when women are let in to an all-male environment, they quickly detect, whether verbally or not, who is gay or not, simply because the lack of erotic tension is such a relief.

The result has been that over the last fifty years or so, particularly in Anglo-Saxon countries, but increasingly obviously everywhere, male groups have found that their togetherness no longer works in the same way. And being male has survived, but changed. One of the results of this has been the ability of some, initially very brave, gay people to say what was previously unimaginable: 'I am', and to get away with it. In other words, the world of mendacity and shaming which bound together the world of same-sex belonging began to collapse, and its collapse was found to be survivable.

Now, here is the problem. The moment some people start to be able to say 'I am' and get away with it, then the grounds are laid for the possibility of simple research as to who such people are, why they are like that, and what it means. I think that we are very early on in our grappling with the possibilities of this sort of research. Such discovery and such research can never advance while the whole area is one of moralising definitions, blaming, togetherness, risk of exposure and of expulsion. Indeed, in this area, as in every other area of human discovery, it has been as we have lost faith in the a priori wickedness of the 'other' that it has become possible to discover what the 'other' really is. To give an example, it wasn't because of the enormous advances in the science of meteorology that people began to doubt whether witches, or the neighbour's evil eye, caused the hailstorm which devastated my crops. It was the loss of faith in the witches being the cause of such things that enabled people to start asking the questions which led to a non-moralistic understanding of meteorology. That is to say it was the discovery of having been wrong about a certain sort of causality which led to the possibility of other sorts of causality being imagined, and thus to our ability to advance in understanding, freedom and responsibility. And this, not as the bright advance of a few brilliant individuals, but as the pacific possession of our race. And by 'pacific possession', I mean something which people cannot go back on in good conscience: anyone who thinks that witches are just as good an explanation of hailstorms as meteorology is either in need of education, or is seeking to do something in bad conscience.

So, a discovery has been made, in large part because of the collapse of entirely false systems of sacrality, concerning a normal part of being human. And that discovery is not in opposition to, but is the fruit of, the process of Christian revelation. It is interesting that those opposed to allowing this discovery to be recognised typically have very little problem with maintaining the old world in which male togetherness went along with male rape and ambiguity and lies concerning gay relationships. Some of the strongest opponents of conceding national and international legal recognition of the humanity of gay people have been those most strongly concerned to maintain a male-only culture, and the Islamic countries are not unique in this regard. It is curious that many of those who claim that the concession of human rights to gay people causes them sleepless nights are caused no insomnia by the massive institutionalised male rape of prison culture. Because 'that's men being men'. Well, it seems to me, from a perusal of Genesis, that if anything deserves to be called colluding with the sin of Sodom, which cries out to heaven for vengeance, it is the colluding in the maintenance of a prison system in which at a conservative estimate there are as many as 900,000 male rapes a year.[2] This is indeed an abomination.

Well, supposing that what I am saying is true, and that it just is the case that we are discovering that there is such a thing as being gay, in itself no moral issue at all, then we can begin to understand both some of the problems which face our Church, and maybe also begin to imagine some of the ways of dealing with them.

If it is true that what has emerged over the last fifty years or so is a collapse of a certain form of male togetherness, and the identities which that engendered, and if it is this which has made it possible to say that there is such a thing as being gay, then it is not surprising that it has had certain consequences. One of these, of direct relevance to our Church's life, has been that what used to be a comparatively safe space, in a very unsafe world, has over a short stretch of time become a very unsafe space. Up until about fifty years ago, the clerical structures of the Catholic Church (and in my country the same would have been true of the Church of England) were probably the safest space within which to be a gay

---

2. From James Gilligan MD, *Violence: Reflections on a National Epidemic* (New York: Vintage, 1996/7), p. 176.

man. That is to say, here was a safe space where it was what you did, not who you were perceived to be, which mattered, and one where you could be decorative, flamboyant, quiet, or whatever, but above all, unmarried, and be respected and not shamed for it. One of the curious things about the present paedophile row is how it contains echoes of earlier rows, for civil society has always been much tougher on 'sodomites' than ecclesiastical courts, and it is a traditional complaint from the Middle Ages and beyond that the Church was far too lenient in its treatment of such people among the clergy. The difference now, curiously, is that the civil courts are able to distinguish perfectly clearly between child abuse and being gay, where it is not at all clear that church authority has been able in practice to make that distinction, because it has so far resisted the discovery of the existence of gay people as a normal part of nature which has become ever clearer in the rest of society.[3]

What has changed in the last fifty years or so is that increasing numbers of people in ordinary civil life, people who are neither special nor distinguished, but ordinary Joes and Jennifers, have been able to say 'I am' and to get away with it. And in our church structure, this has proved to be deeply threatening, because our church structure depends on the old way of being male together, the world of bonding and of shaming, which is both tolerant and violent at the same time. It is notorious in the Church that it is not 'acting out' in same-sex acts which causes trouble, but rather talking about them, or saying 'I am'. That is to say, it is not sex, but honesty which threatens a certain form of being-male-together. But it is the collapse of this whole way of being male together which has allowed the truth that there just *are* gay people to be discovered. And now what used to be an unsafe space, the civil world, has become much safer, while the ecclesiastical world has suddenly become much, much less safe. In fact it imposes an intolerable burden of dishonesty on its gay members, not because it

3. That Archbishop Julian Herranz, head of the Pontifical Council for the Interpretation of Legislative Texts, recently described paedophilia as a 'concrete form of homosexuality' is illustrative of this.

has suddenly become nastier, but because what used to be the only way to survive has now come to seem a form of cowardice kept alive by an institutionalised form of emotional blackmail.

This has led to our trying to cope with that change with entirely inappropriate intellectual tools. For instance, there is no doubt at all that it is a long-standing tradition of the Christian Church to disapprove of sexual acts between males. This tradition has been buttressed by recourse to two sorts of arguments: at a more popular level, by preaching about the sin of Sodom, and the development, or invention as Mark Jordan very properly describes it, of 'sodomy'.[4] Now the notion of sodomy, and along with it of the sodomite, had as one of its effects the description of a being who was 'out there' and who was so strange and bizarre, so dangerous to the realm of nature and order, that for much of the time, ordinary life could go on peacefully, since much of what happened between ordinary Joes or ordinary Jennifers couldn't possibly be sodomy, since they were far too clearly unthreatening to the realm of nature, of royal authority and so on.[5] But the whole point of the term 'sodomite' was that it was a way of referring to a 'them', never to an 'I', and the co-existence of a wicked and outlandish 'them' and all sorts of ordinary same-sex relationships within a world of male bonding was perfectly acceptable. Though there was always the risk, especially higher up the social scale, that as politics and games of power came to matter, so it might become convenient to designate someone as one of 'them' so as to get rid of them. The other sort of argument, of a more professional sort, was the argument which condemned same-sex acts as defections from the proper order of nature, since that was clearly revealed in the reproductive possibilities of marriage between a male and a female. In other words, it was an argument which depended on there being no such thing as a gay person, merely 'straight' people, some of whom might behave badly.

---

4. Mark D. Jordan, *The Invention of Sodomy in Christian Theology* (Chicago: University of Chicago Press, 1997).
5. For examples of how this worked, see Alan Bray's magisterial *Homosexuality in Renaissance England* (New York: Columbia University Press, 1995).

Thus the tools we have had at our disposal have been ones which simultaneously developed a mythical 'they' and reinforced this with a denial of the possibility of there being such a thing as someone who was simply, as a normal part of nature, principally attracted to others of their own gender.

As the world of male togetherness collapsed, and distinctions started to be made, rather than the arguments collapsing, they became more tightly woven together, as the all-male group which is the clerical world in our Church reacted to the threat to its group identity and its credibility. So, gay people continued to be talked about as 'they', using the same mythical and rhetorical structure inherited from the discourse about Sodom, but with a problem. The members of the male group who were using the talk about a 'they' were using it about what was, from the point of view of their male group, a necessary fiction which enabled tolerance within; but they were also applying it to increasing numbers of people both outside and within that group who were able to say 'I am'. And the discourse was never designed for anyone to be able to say 'I am'. It was a victimary discourse, a way of pointing the finger. And of course, increasingly, the younger members of the all-male group could, and can, no longer use the 'they' with good conscience, since they know that the 'they' is in many cases an 'I' and a 'we'.

It is in these circumstances, I think, that we can begin to understand the reactions from the Vatican Congregations from the 1970s onwards, which is the only period in church history from which we have what purports to be a systematic treatment of the gay issue in documents emanating from the Roman Curia. What was not in question, during the time of mendacity, did not need to be taught clearly. But by the 1970s ecclesiastical authorities were faced with a serious problem. They knew that the traditional prohibition was of same-sex *acts*. They probably also knew, since they are not fundamentalists, that the scriptural texts traditionally used to uphold the teaching were not really useful to them, since condemning male rape or sacred prostitution is not the same thing as commenting on consensual adult relations that are part of a partnership. And they also knew that, in Catholic teaching, something is not wrong because it is prohibited, it is prohibited because it is wrong. In other words, for the prohibition to stand, it had to have some basis in the nature of the people involved. The traditional Latin tag is '*agere sequitur esse*' – acting follows from being. If there were such a thing as people who simply are principally attracted to their own gender, then the prohibition could not stand in their case. For they would be acting according to their being. So to recognise the natural existence and moral neutrality of being gay meant that the prohibition could only apply to those for whom it was not natural. Thus they were faced with a dilemma. Either to concede the full humanity of gay people, and drop the prohibition in their case; or to maintain the prohibition, and declare that since it was from God it must correspond to something about the nature of those even for whom it seemed natural. In other words, they were aware that for the prohibition to stand, it had to be shown to be a deduction from a truth about the condition of those involved.

It was, of course, the latter route which they chose (and what else could they do? – they could scarcely say non-procreative sexual acts were valid for gay people, but not for straight people, and Paul VI had just reaffirmed in *Humanae Vitae* the traditional prohibition on straight sexual acts which separate the procreative from the unitive). Thus we were treated to an amazing innovation in teaching, an official attempt to characterise gay people in such a way as to maintain the prohibition but without saying anything at all empirically verifiable (and thus empirically challengeable) about gay people. This is the famous teaching that 'the homosexual inclination, though not itself a sin, constitutes a tendency towards behaviour that is intrinsically evil, and therefore must be considered objectively disordered.'

Now I bring this out because it seems to me that one of the important things about this teaching is its quite extraordinary fragility. Effectively it recognises that the whole, and the only, question is about the nature of things. And, for the ecclesiastical prohibition to stand, the nature of things has to be determined from an a priori deduction about the natural order. No verifiability is allowed. No amount of experience or discovery or learning is possible. The nature of things, regardless of what your or my experience teaches, is such and such, and thus behaviour which seems natural, isn't.

To understand this argument better, apply it to the issue of left-handedness. We have discovered that some people just are left-handed. But let us suppose that in our ancient texts we were to have noticed that the right hand is always the favoured one, and the left hand is always used for dishonest purposes (in many cultures it is used for cleaning the behind after defecation, and is thus unclean), and we were to have determined that this was a clear indication of the divine order of the world. Imagine, as was the case, that with this in mind, left-handed people were mistreated, subjected to corrective learning and so on so as to make them right-handed. And then imagine that some people started to insist on the naturalness and moral irrelevance of being left-handed, and when allowed to flourish as such were able to write left-handedly, play tennis left-handedly, cut cloth left-handedly and so on, and even, horror of horrors, went so far as to lobby for manufacturers to design left-handed scissors, and other implements for their convenience. Well, you can imagine what the doyens of the sacred order would have to do. Either they would have to concede that there just is such a thing as left-handedness, revise the cultural relativity of their sacred texts, and let people get on with it, or they would have to say something rather like this: 'You may think you are left-handed, but that is a deep lie; your being is profoundly right-handed, and it is only if you behave right-handedly that you will flourish. There is a deep metaphysical right-handedness in your being, which is part of the order of creation, unknown to you, and incapable of being verified, such that even if you seem to be flourishing more when acting as if being left-handed were natural, you are gravely self-deceived, and must not listen to those who would tempt you to believe in your just being left-handed. We know more than you about the truth of your being, and we know it from God.'

I hope the parallel is obvious. We would say: well, it is the flourishing which determines the rightness, not the deep and hidden metaphysical claim, for the latter is an a priori, and a way of trying to make reality stay within a particular framework, rather than simply accepting that we can learn that our particular framework is inadequate to reality. And we would be more Catholic in associating God with the flourishing than those who associated God with a metaphysical a priori, because we would be recognising that natural law is the way verifiability challenges metaphysical a prioris, and thus saves our Church from becoming a sacred sect, defined by bizarre and anti-rational taboos.

However, I would like to point out something more about the innovative official characterisation of gay people. It also serves a social function within the all-male group. It is meant to work as a way of keeping alive the old male-togetherness mode of bonding because, following on from the rhetoric of Sodom, it manages to keep alive the mythical 'they', but simultaneously introject it into the 'I' of a person. It is thus the coming together of a violent form of rhetoric and an a priori deduction, and is intellectually scandalous because of the one (the a priori deduction) and morally scandalous because of the other (the demand that I treat my 'I' as though it had within it an evil 'they', and the claim that God so regards me). This is, quite literally, the demand for a sacrifice necessary to maintain a system of mendacity.

This is the double bind with which gay men, and I do not know whether I speak for lesbian women, have been living within the Church at least during my lifetime. The tension between, on the one hand, gradually learning that being able to say 'I am', and so to live, is the path to flourishing, and on the other, the indication that to say 'I am' is to deny God. Luckily, this tension, and with it the teaching, is breaking down.

And indeed, all the signs are that the field of mendacity which we have inherited, and not had the tools to work through, is beginning to unravel before our eyes. I don't know whether you've ever been in an earthquake. I have, on several occasions. The first one I remember as a curious experience. First there was a moment of dizziness, in which I thought that I must be about to faint. Then I realised that the dizziness was because the floor was moving, not I. Then there was a moment of panic as I realised the danger I was in. And then, almost immediately, I realised that whatever this earthquake thing was, it was so big, so much outside my power to do anything about, that I might as well relax and enjoy the ride. And so I did. I feel rather the same about the forces shaking our Catholic world at the moment. I'm sorry for those caught on the outer edge of the earthquake – those who were abused, their abusers and those whose culture of mendacity prepared them only to cover up for these latter, but I'm enjoying the ride, scary, humbling, and sometimes stomach-churning though it be. Something much bigger than us is shaking us up, and the result can only be better than what went before. It is some-thing which, with hindsight, has been coming these twenty years or more, and the attempts to batten down the hatches and forbid discussion have all proved, however well-intentioned they may have been, heroic failures.

Well, I'd like, within this earthquake, to insist on one simple thing, and some of its consequences. The only question at stake for the Church on the gay issue is the following: either there is or there isn't such a thing as being gay as a normal and unremarkable part of nature. If there isn't, then of course church authority is right to try to get people not to act according to what they are not, and all of its culture of secrecy, tolerance, cover-up and ambi-guity is simply what trying to be merciful looks like in the midst of a world gone mad, which is no doubt how some in authority see it. But if there is, then we are in for a time of pain as it becomes clear how vital mendacity has been to the structure of our Church. And here I want to take issue with a couple of voices from the Church in the United States who have taken slightly different tacks in their analysis of the problems we face. Donald Cozzens sees the presence of a disproportionate number of gay men in the priesthood as off-putting to the possibility of straight men joining. He indicates that from the perspective of many straight priests, celibacy is optional for gay priests.[6] And indeed, one of the stupidities of our Church in its current mess is that where a stable relationship of marriage, an undisputed good in itself, would probably cause a priest to lose his job, at least

---

6. 'Time to face the facts', *The Tablet* (4 May 2002), pp. 8–9.

in Anglo-Saxon countries,[7] a discreet but stable same-sex relationship, or indeed discreet multiple same-sex relationships, considered by church authority to be bad, can be, and frequently are, overlooked.

Where I challenge Cozzens is in his seeming assumption that this is something to do with being gay, rather than something to do with inhabiting a field of mendacity. No. The question of truth comes first.[8] While church authority is denying reality by indicating that celibacy is the only option for a gay person, then of course you are going to have a world inhabited by people who are there, half as willing and half as emotionally blackmailed, with all the attendant problems which that raises, including the creation of bitchy, codified subcultures, always the sign of people living in enforced infantilism, not free adulthood. But when church authority accepts the truth: that there are some people who are gay, and that their flourishing looks remarkably like that of straight people, then you will not get seminaries full of people whose relationship to celibacy is deeply, and understandably, ambiguous. Some honest gay men who find themselves called to celibacy will join up. Just as some honest straight men do. And neither will put the other off. For the moment, the twin forces of the non-acceptance of the anthropological reality of gay people, and the obligation of celibacy, serve to create a deeply ambiguous place, a severely queasy mentality, and one which would, I hope, put off anyone who was honest. But the solution to the problem lies in the recognition that the virtue of chastity, which is arduously acquired singleness of heart, and which I take to be an indispensable part

---

7. Though I am aware that a 'don't ask, don't tell' policy is operative with some straight priests in long-term relationships, that there are a large number of women in long-term relationships with priests who experience the Church as a form of wife-abuse, and of course that there is an entirely legitimate presence within the Catholic presbyterate of former Anglican and other Protestant ministers who were already married within their previous affiliations.

8. Cozzens comes close to acknowledging this in his book *Sacred Silence: Denial and Crisis in the Church* (Collegeville: The Liturgical Press, 2002), published after this chapter was written.

of what the reception of salvation looks like in any Christian life, means learning 'my body given for you' rather than 'your body taken for me' in whatever circumstances we find ourselves, over time. For gay people just as for straight people. That is all. In short, getting the official teaching made adequate to discovered reality is a necessary first step towards making of the priesthood an honest profession.

However, I would also like to take issue with some who, in order to defend gay clergy against what they perceive to be an attack by Donald Cozzens, emphasise that such is the clerical power structure that it is no wonder that we gay clergy live dishonest lives if we are to survive. I think that this defence does no favours to gay clergy. Of course power structures favour mendacity, but surely the mendacity of power cannot be allowed to be an excuse for the dishonesty of gay people within the clerical system? No Christian can ever *justify* their dishonesty by blaming power. Our religion is specifically about someone who gave his life so as to make the truth shine in the midst of the mendacity of power. Not to be able to stand up for truth may be understandable, and for many of us, learning to be able to tell the truth at all has been a slow and painful process. But not standing up, over time, for what you know to be the truth can never be *justified*. And in any case, it is important that we remember that in the light of the death and resurrection of our Lord, the worldly power which works by scapegoating and mendacity has been shown to have been overcome. It is a pathetic mirage which roars loudly so as to hide its feebleness. In truth, what could be more pathetic, and less powerful, than these broken old men, our brothers, going down to their graves in shame, apparently unable to understand what has happened, or how the machine which they saw themselves as serving to the best of their ability, has swallowed them and given them not the persona of a child of God, but the mask of a failed corporate manager?

No, it is by standing up for what is, enduring the cross and despising the shame, that we get to make the truth resplendent, confident that loss of job, of reputation, of security and so forth is not an optional extra, but is just part of what being Christian means. If we are to be a minister, either we will be one of Christ, or one of the machine, but we can never blame the machine for not allowing us to be a minister of Christ. Rather we must laugh at it, tolerantly, and with a certain debonair quality as we go about the task of trying to give a soft landing to those it has trapped into being unable to imagine how loved they are, and who fear to receive that love. Then we will be able, after all, to share together in the great rejoicing.

unbinding the gay conscience

introduction

I would like to begin by telling you a bit about my friend Benjamin O'Sullivan. Benjamin was a Benedictine monk of Ampleforth Abbey who killed himself early in 1996. As far as I can tell, he was set up by a reporter from a tabloid newspaper, and the only thing which prevented his death from being a murder was that Benjamin himself consented to the voice of the lynch mob and became the hand that put him to death. I felt that his death was brought about because this extremely attractive, apparently self-confident, effervescent young man had been unable to stand up as an ordinary gay man to the voice of the lynch mob. And the reason he had been unable to stand up to them was because he was bound in his conscience. Shortly after his ordination he had expressed a fear to me that he wasn't really a priest, because 'if they had known', surely they wouldn't have ordained him. That hardly anyone who knew Benjamin well can have failed to know that he was gay is of course not relevant: the person caught in the trap looks at the world through fear-coloured spectacles, and fear darkens rather than illumines what it projects. But this gives a hint of what I mean by a bound conscience: the sort of person who can't stand up and be what they are, who can't trust in the good-ness of what they are being given to become, whatever the lynch mob may throw at them, the sort of person who labours instead in a world of half-truths, any belonging being a half-belonging, because always feeling that 'if they knew' then 'I wouldn't really be allowed here'. Which translates into a permanent and deep feeling of 'I'm not really allowed here'.

It seemed to me, and seems to me, and I told this to Cardinal Hume when I visited him to talk about Benjamin sometime later, that the fact that the Church can no longer easily say, as Peter could to the man lame from birth at the Beautiful Gate in Acts 3, 'In the name of Jesus of Nazareth, walk' is, while sad, something I can live with. But if the Church, and by that I mean if *we*, cannot even unbind a conscience like Benjamin's, then we really are fit for nothing more than to be thrown out and trodden under foot like the saltless salt we are become.

I realised, after this, that given that our hierarchs were not going to do anything, in fact, probably are not able to do anything, paralysed themselves so often by the same bound conscience which afflicted Benjamin, I had to write something which would contribute to the unbinding of the gay conscience, try to find the other-given authority to be able to say 'In the name of Jesus of Nazareth, stand and be.' And the result of my failure to do that in a systematic way is to be found in a book called *Faith beyond Resentment: Fragments Catholic and Gay*.[1]

All I could do in that book was come up with some signposts to my sense that if the Jesus of the gospels really is alive and in our midst, and if he really is what God's self-disclosure to us looks like, then unbinding the gay conscience is very much the sort of thing that he finds himself doing here and now. He is God's pastoring of the sheep whom the shepherds have abandoned, and it does make sense to work out what that looks like.

If the question, then, is not 'what would Jesus do?' but 'what is Jesus doing?' (and I take it that the latter is the authentically Catholic question, presupposing the real presence of Jesus in an ongoing project, rather than a textual presence in a receding past), then it makes sense to spend a little time reflecting on the power of the One who unbinds our conscience.

Let me say first that in an ideal world, Peter would realise that he had been given the power to bind and loose specifically so as to be able to open heaven to the gentiles. He would pronounce those words, 'God has shown me that I should not call any human

---

1. London: Darton, Longman & Todd/New York: Crossroad, 2001.

profane or impure,'[2] and gay people would find themselves with unbound conscience as brothers and sisters in the Church on the same footing as everyone else, that is to say, as sons and daughters and heirs.

But in fact, it seems to me that we find ourselves in a strange moment in that story from Acts 10. We find ourselves in the tiny gap *after* Peter has preached to us about Jesus, whom God anointed with the Holy Spirit and power,[3] *after* we have believed that message, and so realise that Jesus is Good News for us, and *after* the Holy Spirit has come down upon us, so that we are beginning to live the life of loved children and are able to speak well of God.[4] But we find ourselves in the tiny space *before* Peter has found it in him to declare '"Can any one forbid water for baptizing these people who have received the Holy Spirit just as we have?" And he commanded them to be baptized in the name of Jesus Christ.'[5]

If you want a reality check on this, then consider what the current teaching of the Vatican Congregations is: 'The homosexual inclination, though not itself a sin, constitutes a tendency towards behaviour that is intrinsically evil, and therefore must be considered objectively disordered.' If you read that phrase in the light of the passage from Acts which I have just recalled, you can see quite clearly that it is a piece of backsliding. Where Peter said, 'God has shown me that I should not call any human profane or unclean', his current representatives say, 'While it is true that gay people are not profane or unclean, they must in fact be considered to be so.'

So, we find ourselves living at a time of Petrine backsliding from the Gospel, and yet beginning to be aware that the reception of the Good News, and our own unbinding, does not come from Peter, but from God, and that Peter later on gets to understand and confirm this. This is a perfectly understandable biblical pattern which we can inhabit while we wait for Peter.

---

2. Acts 10:28.
3. Acts 10:34–43.
4. Acts 10:44–6.
5. Acts 10:47–8.

Now what I would like to do today is start to examine the binding and the unbinding. What does it look like? I suppose the first step is to look at what being 'bound' means. A bound conscience is one which cannot go this way or that, forwards or backwards, is paralysed, scandalised. In that sense it is a form of living death, and those afflicted by it are living dead, and many of us are or have been such people. Let me give some examples of what I mean. We are familiar with the notion of a 'double bind' or a 'Catch-22 situation'. A bound conscience is a sense of being formed by a double bind or a series of double binds. For instance: 'My command is that you should love, but your love is sick'; or 'You should just go away and die, but it is forbidden to kill yourself'; or 'The only acceptable way for me to live is a celibate life, but if they knew who I really was, they wouldn't allow me to join'; or 'Of course you can join, but you mustn't say who you really are'; or 'You cannot be gay, but you must be honest.' Many of us have been inducted into just such patterns of desire over time. They classically follow the form 'Imitate me, do not imitate me.' If you find yourself gravitationally pulled towards someone, and yet the message given to you is 'Be like me, do not be like me', you will be scandalised, and eventually you will judder to a halt, unable to move forwards or backwards.

What I would like to suggest is that in all these cases we are dealing with a self that has been formed by being given contradictory desires without being given any ability to discern where those desires might appropriately be applied. In other words, two instructions are received as on the same level as each other, pointing in two different directions at once, and the result is paralysis. This is what σκάνδαλον – *skandalon* – refers to in the New Testament: scandal, or stumbling block. Someone who is scandalised is someone who is paralysed into an inability to move. And the undoing of σκάνδαλα – *skandala* – which means the unbinding of double binds that do not allow people to be, is what the Gospel is supposed to be about.

I want to make it quite clear that we are dealing with something very basic and central to the Gospel here. It is perfectly possible to present the Gospel in such a way that it is a sort of double bind. Any sort of presentation of the Christian faith which says 'I love you but I do not love you', or 'I don't love you as you are, but if you become someone different I will love you', is in fact preaching a double bind, a stumbling block, a pathway to paralysis.

Let's imagine the conversation between a false god and the self:

False god: I want to love you, but I can't love you as you are, because you are sinful and objectively disordered.
Self: Well, what then must I do to be loved?
False god: You must become someone different.
Self: I'm up for it, show me how.
False god: Love isn't something that can be earned, it just is.
Self: Well then, how do I get to become the sort of person who can be loved?
False god: If I were you I would start somewhere else.
Self: That's a great help. How do I start somewhere else?
False god: You can't, because even starting off *for* somewhere else starts *from* you, and you can't be loved.
Self: Well, if I can't start off from somewhere else, and I can't start off from where I am, what can I do?
False god: Give up on the love thing; just obey and be paralysed.

That's how powerful it is to receive our sense of self, our identity, our desire, in imitation of, through the regard of, eyes which give us a mixed message, a double bind.

Now if the Gospel means anything at all it means that the Good News about God is unambivalent, that there are no 'ifs and buts' in God – God's love is unconditional. And this means, above all, that there are no double binds in God. God desires that our desire should flow free, life-giving and untrammelled, because it is in that flow of desire that we are called into being.

Well, if that is the case, imagine then what might be a conversation between the unambivalently loving God and the self:

Unambivalently loving God: I love you.
Self: But I'm full of shit. How can you love me?
Unambivalently loving God: I love you.

Self: But you can't love me – I'm part of all this muck.

Unambivalently loving God: It's you that I love.

Self: How can it be me that you love when I've been involved in bad relationships, dark rooms, machinations against other people?

Unambivalently loving God: It's you that I love.

Self: But . . .

Unambivalently loving God: It's you that I love.

Self: But . . .

Unambivalently loving God: It's you that I love.

Self: OK then, so are you just going to leave me in the shit?

Unambivalently loving God: Because I love you you are relaxing into my love and you will find yourself becoming lovable, indeed becoming someone that you will scarcely recognise.

Self: Hadn't I better do something to get all ready for this becoming lovable?

Unambivalently loving God: Only if you haven't yet got it that it's I who do the work and you who get to shine. Because I love you, you are relaxing into being loved and will find yourself doing lovable things because you are loved.

Self: I think I could go along with this.

Or to put it in a nutshell, when faced with the standard Irish joke about 'How do I get to Dublin?' and being told 'If I were you I wouldn't start from here', the Gospel response, that is to say the regard of Christ, tells us: 'I will come with you starting from where you are.'

Now I put it to you as a question: is the teaching of the Vatican Congregations which I quoted to you before compatible with the Gospel, or is it compatible with the bad Irish joke? I'll quote it for you again: 'The homosexual inclination, though not itself a sin, constitutes a tendency towards behaviour that is intrinsically evil, and therefore must be considered objectively disordered.'

To me at least it is clear. This teaching is interposing itself between the regard of Christ and our own sense of being, in a way which tends to pervert the simple regard of one who loves us as we are, and as loved we will find ourselves becoming someone different. It is teaching us instead that God will only love us if we start from somewhere else. That is to say, the teaching is in the technical sense a *skandalon*, a stumbling block, something which compounds a double bind rather than undoing it. It is because I think that the teaching is incompatible with the Gospel at this very fundamental level that I also think that, despite the protestations of the current office-holders in the Roman Curia, it cannot in fact be the teaching of the Church.

A dimension of this which I have brought out more or less strongly, and which may not be obvious when people talk about conscience,[6] is the importance of understanding that our conscience is *always* related to and formed by what is other than us, prior to us, outside us. It is not as though there is a 'real' private voice somewhere inside us which gives us infallible deliverances which are right. On the contrary, what constitutes our 'inside' is a more or less well-managed conversation between different voices which have called us into being one way or another, through parents, education, Church, politicians, and which often enough have tied us up. We are called into being as bodies acting in the world through those voices. This means that when it comes to the unbinding of conscience, it is not ever a question of searching back under all the voices for some innocent voice which I know to be a 'good conscience'. That is merely a terrible form of self-deception. No, both the being given a self and a sense of self through language, and the unbinding of the conscience, are always the work of someone else, outside us, and the most important thing is 'to which other are we listening?' Who is the 'other' who can unbind our conscience, who can induct us into desiring without double binds?

I rather suspect that this helps to bring out part of the impression which Jesus left on those to whom he spoke, and is therefore rather the impression that he leaves when he speaks to us: 'for he taught them as one who had authority, not as the scribes',[7] or 'my sheep hear my voice, and I know them, and they

---

6. See note at end of this chapter.
7. Matt. 7:29; Mark 1:22.

follow me.'[8] Speaking with authority means speaking from within the power of the author, the beginner, the Creator, and can be recognised precisely because it unbinds double binds and stumbling blocks which cannot be from God because no good Creator could possibly treat his creatures in this way.

I would like to dwell a little more on the effects on us of this regard, the one which looks at us and says 'I love you, and as you discover yourself loved you will find yourself becoming something else.' I want to say something apparently rather banal here, but I think it is rather important. I think that we would be wise to send the word 'love' to the laundry and use the word 'like' instead. I say this for the following reason. You have probably met people, as I have, who tell us that they love gay people, and that is why they are so keen to change us. In other words their 'love' does not include the word 'like'. It means something like: 'I feel that in obedience to God's love for sinners I must stop you being who you are.'

But in fact the word 'like' is rather more difficult to twist into a lie than the word 'love', because we know when someone likes us. We can tell because they enjoy being with us, alongside us, want to share our time and company. Well, what I would like to suggest is that if our understanding of being loved does not include being liked, or at least being prepared to learn to be liked, then there's a good chance that we're talking about the sort of love that can slip a double bind over us, that is really saying to us 'My love for you means that I will like you if you become someone else.'

It seems to me that the doctrine of the incarnation of our Lord, the image of God coming among us as the likeness of humans,[9] is a strong statement that the divine regard is one of *liking* us, here and now, as we are. Glad to be with us. And this means that the one who looks at us with love is not just looking at us with a penetrating and inscrutable gaze of utter otherness, but is looking at us with the delight of one who enjoys our company, who wants

8. John 10:27.
9. Phil. 2:7.

to be one with us, to share in something with us. Sure, as we learn to relax into that being loved, we are going to find that we are quite different from what we thought we were, and that our patterns of desire will become quite different, which is what it means to find that the Holy Spirit has come to dwell in us in and through the reformation of our desire. But the regard does not first knock down so as then to build up, as we so often imagine it, rather as though Jesus was a sergeant-major whose job it is to give hell to the recruits and make them feel awful so that later, after they've lost their identities, they'll start to feel good new identities as soldiers, and then they'll discover that the 'sarge' has a heart of gold.

No, our faith is that the eyes of God that are in Christ, and thus the divine regard through which we can receive new being, are eyes that like us, from alongside, at the same level as us. Which means, they do not control us, do not try to 'know better than us' who we are, but want to participate in a discovery with us of who we are to become.

And that means that there is no plot to lose. There is only an adventure of trusting in the goodness of the one who loves us and seeing what we would really like to do.

Our Lord put it this way:

> "For it will be as when a man going on a journey called his servants and entrusted to them his property; to one he gave five talents, to another two, to another one, to each according to his ability. Then he went away. He who had received the five talents went at once and traded with them; and he made five talents more. So also, he who had the two talents made two talents more. But he who had received the one talent went and dug in the ground and hid his master's money. Now after a long time the master of those servants came and settled accounts with them. And he who had received the five talents came forward, bringing five talents more, saying, 'Master, you delivered to me five talents; here I have made five talents more.' His master said to him, 'Well done, good and faithful servant; you have been faithful over a little, I will set you over much;

enter into the joy of your master.' And he also who had the two talents came forward, saying, 'Master, you delivered to me two talents; here I have made two talents more.' His master said to him, 'Well done, good and faithful servant; you have been faithful over a little, I will set you over much; enter into the joy of your master.' He also who had received the one talent came forward, saying, 'Master, I knew you to be a hard man, reaping where you did not sow, and gathering where you did not winnow; so I was afraid, and I went and hid your talent in the ground. Here you have what is yours.' But his master answered him, 'You wicked and slothful servant! You knew that I reap where I have not sowed, and gather where I have not winnowed? Then you ought to have invested my money with the bankers, and at my coming I should have received what was my own with interest. So take the talent from him, and give it to him who has the ten talents. For to every one who has will more be given, and he will have abundance; but from him who has not, even what he has will be taken away. And cast the worthless servant into the outer darkness; there men will weep and gnash their teeth.'''[10]

The key feature of this parable is that it is the imagination of the servants as to what their master is like which is the determining factor of their conscience and thus the wellspring of their activity. The first two servants clearly imagined their master being away as an opportunity to do something delightful. They trusted that their master was the sort of daring fellow who would do rash and crazy things for which there was no script, would dare, would experiment, would risk losing things and so would end up multiplying things greatly. In other words, they perceived their master's regard for them as one of liking them enough to be daring them and encouraging them to be adventurous, and so, imagining and trusting that abundance would multiply, they indeed multiplied abundance. The third servant revealed exactly what regard he had laboured under: his imagination of who the master is comes out

---

10. Matt. 25:14–30.

in his own words: 'Master, I knew you to be a hard man, reaping where you did not sow, and gathering where you did not winnow; so I was afraid, and I went and hid your talent in the ground.' He acted according to his imagination. And his imagination was one of a double bind, perfectly captured in the phrase 'reaping where you did not sow, and gathering where you did not winnow'. His perception of the other was of one who did not like him and thus had put an impossible burden on him, and so all he had done was simply sulk. He had been bound, the living dead, moving neither forward nor backward. It is no wonder that in Luke's version, the master says 'Out of your own mouth I will condemn you, you wicked servant',[11] because it is in fact the servant's own perception that has bound him.

Now I put it to you that the eucharistic presence of Jesus in our midst is the way God constantly reminds us, calls us into mind, of his regard, one of liking us, encouraging us to be daring with him, during the time of the 'absence of the master', and that our having our conscience unbound means our becoming able to trust in the regard of one who likes us and so is delighted that we will come up with crazy new daring schemes which didn't seem to be part of the programme at all. And it is according to our conscience that we will act. If our conscience accepts the regard of, and wants to be like, someone who likes us, who is daring, creative, innovative, effervescent, unafraid, risk-taking and so on, then we will find ourselves behaving like that, being able to stand up and take the rap, delighting in finding ways of getting people off the hook, never taking no for an answer, refusing to believe that something is impossible for God; and that is who we will become.

Someone of unbound conscience can dare to get it wrong, because they don't have to get it right. If you have to get it right, that means that you don't dare to get it wrong, which means that you are afraid of what will happen to you if you do get it wrong. But the Catholic and Christian understanding of conscience is that because we know that we are liked we can get it wrong, and it

---

11. Luke 19:22.

doesn't matter, because we are not frightened of punishment, but able to learn from our mistakes. In fact, if we can't dare to be wrong, then we can't truly get it right, because our being right will be a form of protection against what is other than us, what is unknown, exciting, big and causing us to be bigger-minded, magnanimous. A good conscience is not a feeling of self-satisfaction at having got it right; it is much more the underlying excitement of knowing yourself on the way somewhere, which is perfectly compatible with a deep sorrow of realisation at having got something wrong. This is the excitement of being a son or daughter who is on an adventure, not the contractual precision of a slave who has to get something right because he has no sense of being on the inside of the project of whoever is in charge, and merely senses the other as arbitrary and capricious, as someone who will glower at what is not perfect.

Well, what does it mean to you that God does not merely 'love' us gay people in a clinical, arms-length sense, but likes us, enjoys our company, wants to be in on the adventure with us, see where we can take the adventure of being human? Is it not true that the mere phrase 'I like you' gives permission to be, is creative of space, suggests 'I'm curious to accompany you', means delight? And if that is the case, why don't we dare to imagine that God does actually want us to be free and happy, starting exactly from where we are; that our desire for a loving partner, or to build a crazy community project full of eccentric queens making a difference to society and Church, is something which could well lead to fulfilment, a fulfilment much bigger than we could imagine. Just because Peter hasn't yet got it, doesn't mean that the Spirit can be stopped from unbinding our desire. Just because some of our hierarchs seem unable to dare even to offer us the sort of eucharistic space which is our baptismal new-birthright doesn't mean that our consciences need be bowed down by, bound by, all that heaviness of decline management, that defensive bureaucratic inability to negotiate as adults with adults. For that heaviness and that inability says something about them, and need say nothing about us.

Consciences are unbound for a doing and a becoming, and that,

I think, is where we find ourselves now: given that the only judgement we will receive will be that of freedom,[12] what do we want to dare to do, starting now? What would it be fun to present our master with on his return?

One final point. I think we are very privileged to be gay and lesbian Catholics at this time, and this is in part because of the growing sense that we are in on the inner dynamic of the project which is the sharing of the Good News about God with the world. I want to point out that one of the features of the texts of the apostolic witnesses in the New Testament is that they are marked to a very strong degree by the notion of a sort of 'coming out', a leaving behind something which, while theoretically good in itself, had turned into a trap. Sometimes this is presented in a moralistic (and indeed anti-Semitic) way as people leaving something bad to join something good. Well, I think it is much closer to the mark to see it as people leaving something apparently 'good' – whether the 'Law' or the decencies of Roman civil religion – and instead becoming free. Paul is keen that the freedom not turn into licentiousness, but he is much, much more keen that people don't go back into 'goodness' with its bound consciences and its comforting dependency on group approval.[13] Which of the following two propositions do you think is closer to the witness of the New Testament?

> A gay Catholic holds that 'not going back like a dog to its vomit'[14] means, first and foremost, not going back to gay meeting places, relationships, places where there is a risk of sex.

Or:

> A gay Catholic holds that 'not going back like a dog to its vomit' means, first and foremost, refusing the lure of the ecclesiastical closet which binds conscience and makes people

12. Jas. 2:12.
13. Gal. 3:1.
14. Cf. Prov. 26:11 and 2 Peter 2:22.

unfree, leading to dysfunctional relations and an inability to love and to tell the truth.

What does the teaching about not putting new wine in old wine-skins, or about avoiding the leaven of the pharisees, mean if it isn't part of the way the author of all things speaks into being a daring conscience?

So, where shall we take it?

Here are some resources for further reading on questions of conscience:

H. Richard Niebuhr, 'The ego–alter dialectic and the conscience', *Journal of Philosophy* 42 (1945), pp. 352–9.

J. Ratzinger, 'Conscience and truth' in John M. Haas (ed.), *Crisis of Conscience* (New York: Crossroad, 1996), pp. 1–20.

H. McCabe, 'Aquinas on good sense' in *God Still Matters* (London: Continuum, 2002), pp. 152–65.

J. Milbank, 'Can morality be Christian?' in *The Word Made Strange* (Oxford: Blackwell, 1997), pp. 219–32.

the importance of being indifferent

Le héros souterrain est un être fasciné qui s'écrase piteusement et tragiquement sur tous les obstacles qui se trouvent sur son chemin, à l'instar du papillon de nuit qui se brûle à la lampe ou de deux Boeings s'encastrant dans les tours de la puissance, et cela parce qu'ils s'occupent plus de l'obstacle que de l'objet. C'est parce que l'orgueil de l'homme du sous-sol est sans limites qu'il peut s'abaisser de la façon la plus abjecte. L'orgueil, et non pas l'égoïsme; la haine de soi, et non pas l'amour de soi. 'Craignons celui qui se hait lui-même, avertit Nietzsche, cet autre grand spécialiste de la psychologie souterraine, car nous serons les victimes de sa vengeance.' [1]

Jean-Pierre Dupuy
'Rousseau et Dostoïevski à Manhattan'

It is difficult to think of any subject which has been more used

---

1. Jean-Pierre Dupuy, *Avions-nous oublié le mal?* (Paris: Bayard, 2002), p. 42. 'The underground hero is someone trapped in fascination who crashes, pitifully and tragically, into all the obstacles to be found in his path, just like a moth which burns itself against a light bulb, or two Boeings embedding themselves in the towers of domination. They do these things because they are more concerned with the obstacle than with the object. It is because the pride of the one who dwells in the underground is limitless that he can abase himself in such an abject manner. Pride and not egoism; self-hatred, and not love of self. "We should fear the person who hates himself" warned Nietzsche, that other great connoisseur of underground psychology, "for we will be the victims of his vengeance." ' (My translation.)

and abused than ecclesiastical language about sheep and shepherds – to such an extent that the very language of the Good Shepherd seems coated in kitsch, and, in the light of recent events in the United States and elsewhere, tinged with a sad, and sometimes appalling, irony.

Nevertheless, I want to have a go at recovering some of the sense of this language as a critical tool with which we can begin to see our way forward and flex our imaginations a little as to what we might be doing in exercising ministry as gay and lesbian people, or for gay and lesbian people.

In the first place, a personal consideration, so as to enable you to reject, if you wish, everything I say hereafter. I am deeply committed to this language of sheep and shepherd, not merely because I am, and am delighted to be, a somewhat traditional Catholic; not merely because the sacred texts in which I dwell, and which I love, cause me to think in their terms; but because my experience has been one of being called into being through the phrase 'Feed my sheep' such that I cannot make sense of my life except as an aspiring to make that summons flesh.

Let me explain. Eight years ago, while on an Ignatian retreat in downtown Santiago in Chile, I underwent something like a 'collapse of world'. Following a particularly nasty outbreak of ecclesiastical homophobia which came my way, my sense of belonging to a religious order, and my way of being part of the Church, were being completely reformulated. This happened as I received the grace of seeing that God has nothing at all to do with the violence which is meted out to gay people, that it is purely a human mechanism. And I was becoming able to detect the ways in which I had been complicit with that violence and those mechanisms owing to living with a bound conscience. At one stage during the tumult of this week-long retreat, I went walking in the early afternoon in one of the gay cruising areas of Santiago, which is also a popular walking spot, and watched a young man looking for a pick-up. I remember thinking that he was probably a soldier, since I had been told that Thursday was when the conscripts had their afternoon off, and the density of military-looking young men would mysteriously increase in the cruising area on that day.

Thinking to myself on my return to the Jesuit house where I was staying that such an afternoon walk was scarcely a proper way to be going about my guided retreat, I spent time in the presence of the Blessed Sacrament. And at some stage the words 'Feed my sheep' came to me, not from my own perturbance, but from Another, resounding like a gentle kettledrum in a silence beneath the jangling of a drum-less orchestra. And this of course threw me completely. Gradually, but completely. Since it seemed to suggest that my afternoon walk was not only one of mixed motives, as I would have been happy to admit, but that there was a loving regard for the men on that mound that had no mixed motives, and simply liked them.

I suppose it has taken me much of the eight years since that event to get some sense of what that regard is about. I notice that it seemed to be part of two experiences. The first was that of a radical separation of God from all the violence; the second was the seriously destabilising possibility of the divine regard looking on gay and lesbian people not with a frisson of disgust marked by condescension, but rather with straightforward liking, and wanting to create a shepherding for us, wanting us to be happy and free, as you do with someone you actually like. The first was the stripping away of something, and the second was the emerging of something different, a perspective which had simply been unimaginable from within the violence. Over time, I see of course that these are the same experience, and that it is the emergence of the gently positive regard which is what leads to the radical separation, even though these may be experienced in the reverse order.

Part of the disconcerting nature of this phrase 'Feed my sheep' was that I understood at once that it did not answer in any way the formal question which I was asking during the retreat, which was whether I really had a vocation to the Dominicans, or instead to the Jesuits, or whether I should really continue to be a priest at all. The resounding phrase was, as a very wise Benedictine friend pointed out to me, 'wonderfully non-directive'. And, at the same time as it was an order which cannot be refused, it was gently inviting of creativity and discovery as to what it might mean. This is the sense in which I cannot let the phrase 'Feed my sheep' go. I am peripheral to the phrase, whoever I am, and in its working out, I will be discovered to be. I have a vague sense that something like this is behind the notion of the ontological character conferred by the sacrament of order, but I may well be wrong about that.

Anyhow, the point of my sharing this with you is that I imagine that if I have had such an experience, then probably many others have had it as well. And such are some of you, who are responding to calls within your different denominations' reception of the Christian faith. What I want to indicate is that when we talk about ministry for gay people and lesbians, or lesbian and gay people in ministry, we are not talking in the first place about techniques, or ideologies. We are not talking about searching for ecclesiastical approval. We are not talking about 'how far can I go?' or 'how much can I get away with?' We are talking about something much more basic. We are talking about being called by God, the Creator of the universe, which is a certain sort of command, and one which, once heard, cannot be unheard, because along with it there goes the sense that whoever it is that 'I' am to become, that becoming will never, however hard we may run away, or allow ourselves to be seduced by worry or fashion, become disentangled from this being addressed as shepherd-in-potential, which is what suggests forth shepherdliness in us.

Well, many of us, I suspect, get so far, and then become distracted by the apparent impossibility of the calling given the various ecclesiastical set-ups in which we find ourselves. And of course I am speaking here in the first instance from within my own experience as a Catholic, but am aware that in many ways the same issues are at work in the different forms in which Christianity is lived out in our countries at the present time. What I want to do is spend time with you today working to chip away at one of the principal obstacles to our developing healthy ministries aimed at producing healthy, happy and free gay and lesbian multipliers of the divine harvesting. The obstacle is, in a single word: fascination. And the cure is, in a single word: indifference.

In order to try and explain what I mean, I would like to go

back to a very fundamental piece of Catholic ecclesiology, which is the thesis that Jesus founded the Church. What I would like to do is to defend this thesis in a rather strong form by recovering some hints of what Jesus seems to have thought he was doing. Far from this being an exercise in triumphalism, it is an exercise in showing that Catholic ecclesiology, and thus any understanding of ministry, is an understanding of how a new and potentially universal 'we' comes into being which is always held in self-critical movement between the twin poles of the notion of 'Temple' and that of 'Shepherd'.

Let me explain with some background. What I would like to suggest is that Judaism and Christianity are both religions of the collapsing Temple. I mean this in the obvious sense that it was the collapse of the Temple in 587 BC which led to the creation of text-based Judaism, and the collapse of the Temple in AD 70 which led to the creation of rabbinic Judaism. But I include also a less obvious sense, which is that in both cases the collapse was seen not merely as a fact of history to be dealt with regretfully, but actually as part of the way in which God tries to get through to us, as part of God's plan to get us beyond something unworthy of us. This strange, properly Jewish prophetic relationship with the collapsing Temple can be seen in the texts of the apostolic witness to the resurrection, which we call the New Testament, both in the mouth of Jesus' accusers and in Jesus' own words and actions. First, let us step back a bit.

In Ezekiel 33, a fugitive comes from Jerusalem to the group of exiles by the river Chebar in the land of the Chaldeans. He announces the fall of the city, not even bothering to mention the destruction of the Temple. This is not news to Ezekiel, who had already seen God in a vision detaching himself from the Temple and becoming flexible and mobile. It is after this that Ezekiel starts with his prophecy against the shepherds of Israel. The passage is very familiar:

> Ho, shepherds of Israel who have been feeding yourselves! Should not shepherds feed the sheep? You eat the fat, you clothe yourselves with the wool, you slaughter the fatlings; but you

do not feed the sheep. The weak you have not strengthened, the sick you have not healed, the crippled you have not bound up, the strayed you have not brought back, the lost you have not sought, and with force and harshness you have ruled them. So they were scattered, because there was no shepherd; and they became food for all the wild beasts.[2]

Now please notice this, the prophecy is *not* that because these shepherds have failed to feed the sheep, the Temple is going to be destroyed, and the flock of Judah carried off to Babylon. It's a bit late for that. No, this bit of the prophecy is simply the preamble to the real prophecy, it's the criticism of what is past in the light of what the prophet sees as already coming into being, a quite new sort of shepherding, one instigated by God himself.

What the prophet sees as coming into being is something quite new:

> Behold, I, I myself will search for my sheep, and will seek them out. As a shepherd seeks out his flock when some of his sheep have been scattered abroad, so will I seek out my sheep; and I will rescue them from all places where they have been scattered on a day of clouds and thick darkness. And I will bring them out from the peoples, and gather them from the countries, and will bring them into their own land; and I will feed them on the mountains of Israel, by the fountains, and in all the inhabited places of the country. I will feed them with good pasture, and upon the mountain heights of Israel shall be their pasture; there they shall lie down in good grazing land, and on fat pasture they shall feed on the mountains of Israel. I myself will be the shepherd of my sheep, and I will make them lie down, says the Lord GOD. I will seek the lost, and I will bring back the strayed, and I will bind up the crippled, and I will strengthen the weak, and the fat and the strong I will watch over; I will feed them in justice.[3]

---

2. Ezek. 34:2–5.
3. Ezek. 34:11–16

It is this which is the real novelty, and it is in light of what Ezekiel sees as coming to happen in the future, in terms of God himself coming to tend his sheep, that the earlier critique was possible. And in Ezekiel's vision this leads eventually to a new and pure Temple in which God plants the soles of his feet so as to dwell in the midst of his people for ever.[4]

Now the interesting thing about this process in the life of Ezekiel is that until he had been able to develop an extraordinary indifference to the Temple and all that went on in it and around it, an indifference marked by his vision of the Lord gradually detaching himself from the Temple and then abandoning it all together, he had not been able to receive the vision of the Lord shepherding his people himself. In other words, the pre-exilic obsession with the presence of the Lord in the Temple, criticised by Jeremiah as well,[5] had to be worked through completely, and lost, before a new vision of what the Temple was really supposed to be about could be imagined, and thus worked towards. To put this in another way: the notion of 'Shepherd' is always to be understood not just as a nice image among other nice images, but as one that only makes sense *in critical juxtaposition to the notion of 'Temple'*.

I put it to you that what Ezekiel was doing was working through a fascination until he was able to achieve a certain sort of indifference. I want to be clear here about how I am using the word indifference. There is a way of using the word indifference which suggests a somewhat petulant gesture of disregard: 'You leave me cold', said with a flick of the wrist. Indifference can suggest haughtiness, being 'above' something. But I would like to ask you to consider it in a much stricter sense, one which will be familiar to those who know St Ignatius' *Spiritual Exercises*.[6] This is the sense in which something ceases to push any of your buttons either positively or negatively. You are neither repelled by something, nor attracted to it, it is just there, and whether it stays or goes

---

4. Ezek. 43:7.
5. Jer. 7:4.
6. Cf, Principle and Foundation, Exercises 23: 'hacernos indiferentes'.

is something which doesn't matter. And the reason this is so is because your heart is pointing somewhere else, and whatever happens or doesn't happen to this thing, you will in any case have your centre of gravity pulling you in quite a different direction, one which is in no way reactive, but creative of something else.

In this sense, indifference is at least as much a correction of love as it is a correction of hate. And that I think was the case with Ezekiel and the Temple. It was Ezekiel's love for what was being lost, his attachment to something deeply ambiguous, at least as much as his fury at those who were involved in its desecration, which needed to be healed and ordered before he was able to share in the heart of God to see what God wanted to do, and what the real purpose of God's love for his people was.

Now I put it to you that one of the most remarkable, and least remarked on, features of Jesus' acting out, teaching and ministry, several centuries later and in a land marked by a new Temple, is his quite extraordinary indifference towards the Temple. He does not appear in any way fascinated by it, neither attracted nor repelled. It seems to have had no emotional weight for him at all. So entirely free from fascination by it was he that he was able to act out the prophetic gesture of the cleansing of the Temple, thus making present an understanding of Jeremiah 7 and, more importantly of Zechariah 14, where there are no longer any traders in the house of the Lord 'on that day'. He was able both to teach in the Temple and to disregard it. He quite specifically taught his disciples to regard the Temple with sublime indifference, to be deeply unconcerned about whether it stood or fell, and certainly to attribute absolutely no divine significance to its standing or its falling.[7] I wonder whether when he watched the widow putting her mite into the Temple treasury and commented on her generosity, his comment wasn't also tinged with a sense of sorrow at her wasting what little she had on something which was on its way to redundancy.

And I think it is worth stopping to consider how very odd an attitude to the Temple this is. It has in fact been just about possible

7. Mark 13 and parallels.

to tell the story of Jesus without reference to the Temple as anything other than a building which happened to be there. We don't take seriously the accusation that Jesus sought to destroy the Temple and indeed, we often read the New Testament as though the Temple were merely part of the background. But this is very odd if we consider that for those who lived in Jerusalem the Temple must have dominated everything. Not merely because of its size, or the economic importance of the market in sacrificial beasts which it spawned, or indeed because of the smell resulting from blood and carcases.

More important than that, the Temple was the centre of mimetic fascination. What do I mean by that? Well, I mean that it constituted the centre of a pattern of desire which drew people in and gave them a sense of belonging which fused together learning, divinity, national identity, career, money, reputation, and so on. It must indeed have been fascinating. It can easily have become an obsession to watch what was going on, who was in, who was out; which one of the crooked placemen who ran the joint was in which faction, which faction was coming out on top, what this meant for the future of the people, and so on.

Now I put it to you that to have been indifferent to all this in the sense which I have ascribed to Jesus, is something very remarkable. Yet that seems to me to have been the case. In Mark's Gospel Jesus comes into Jerusalem in chapter 11, and then in verse 11, it says: 'And he entered Jerusalem and went into the Temple; and when he had looked round at everything, as it was already late, he went out to Bethany with the twelve.' That is all, no special visitation. Just looked around and left. And the next day his cursing of the fig tree seems to suggest, and was certainly taken by the apostolic group to suggest, that his action of the cleansing in the Temple was to be interpreted as declaring the Temple to be henceforth null and void. Zechariah's 'in that day' had come. In response to Peter's pointing out the blighted fig tree the next day, that is to say, the day after 'in that day', Jesus doesn't appear to answer straight. He gives an answer about prayer which presupposes no longer regarding the Temple as a place of prayer (it had after all been made into a den of thieves, as he had pointed out), but praying 'whenever'. Indeed Jesus' line about 'whoever says to this mountain "Be taken up and cast into the sea"' makes much more sense in this context if the 'this mountain' in question is not any old mountain ambling by on its way to the sea, but *the* mount on which the Temple was built.

Now if all this works by resonance and subtlety in Mark, John spells it all out rather more clearly. He states quite straight-forwardly, in the context of the cleansing of the Temple, that Jesus has come to replace it,[8] that Jesus regarded his programme as one of creating a new Temple in his body. It is why in John's Gospel Jesus is crucified at the time the lambs are being slaugh-tered for the Passover in the Temple. He is the Temple, just as he is the Lamb, just as he is the Priest. What he is also, very directly in John (as by allusion in the synoptic gospels), and this is what I would like to bring out here, is the Good Shepherd who is feeding the sheep.[9] That is to say he sees himself as fulfilling the passage from Ezekiel which I quoted to you earlier. He is the 'I myself will search out my sheep' and he is Shepherd not merely by teaching disregard for the Temple, but by himself becoming the Temple, by himself being the sacrifice which brings to an end the cult of the Temple *as centre of mimetic fascination*.

Notoriously, when in the synoptic gospels Jesus inaugurates the Last Supper, he is doing something very remarkable as a way of interpreting his own forthcoming death. He is inaugurating a new cult in his body which goes the reverse route of the sacrificial process. Where the movement in all religions seems to have gone from human sacrifice to animal sacrifice to lesser forms of sacrifice, Jesus traverses exactly the reverse route. He substitutes a human being at the centre of the cult to be the lamb, and makes the cult unnecessary by showing what it is that we do when we sacrifice. That is: we hide over murder. And he does this so that we never need to sacrifice again. What we do instead is to celebrate the being-set-free from sacrifice by repeating with gratitude the way Jesus chose to make his self-giving apparent, which is simul-

8. John 2:13–22.
9. John 10 but see also Matt. 9:36; 10:6; Mark 6:34; etc.

taneously not a sacrifice at all, in the world-religions sense of the word, and the one true sacrifice, since it blows apart the world of sacrifice.

From now on the Temple is wherever ordinary human beings are engaged together in prayer, in treating each other in a way which builds up, and wherever they are together undoing the world of violent sacrifice.

Now what I want to bring out here, and have done so far too sketchily, is something which I think to be of very great importance for those of us who are working at imagining a ministry for gay and lesbian people, or indeed exercising ministry as gay and lesbian people. The Church is founded in a certain sort of deliberate creating of an unimagined new Temple by someone whose imagination was free to create this radically new understanding of a shepherding of God's people. And his imagination was free because it was absolutely untouched by, unshaded by, uninfected by, fascination with the sacred mimetic centre which seemed to so many of his contemporaries to be so redolent of the mystery of God's presence. And as with any such centre of mimetic fascination, it was simultaneously something which drew people in and repelled them. Jesus was entirely free of that. Free to let the Temple be, to declare it desolate, and instead to lead people into something which was perfectly compatible with Temple worship while the Temple was around, but in whose light Temple worship was of fading importance, so that when there was no longer a Temple there, there was no need to reinvent it, since 'the newer rite is here'.

What I want to emphasise is quite what a remarkable, and apparently secularising move this is, this relocation of the Temple onto Jesus' own body, the replacement of Temple sacrifice with a single human 'sacrifice' to be re-presented continuously as a way of inhabiting the time in which the sacred is in perpetual collapse; and quite how deliberate this move of Jesus seems to have been.[10]

Well, does it need me to spell out the point? I think we find ourselves inhabiting just the dynamic which Jesus inaugurated,

---

10. John 10:17–18.

calmly and deliberately, of living in sight of the collapsing Temple while acting with deep indifference to it as he went about the shepherding of his sheep whom the false shepherds and hirelings had abandoned.

Now: how we understand what Jesus is doing here is, I think, of vital importance for fundamental ecclesiology, and therefore for the root understanding of any of our ministries. If we see Jesus as in some way 'dissing' the Temple establishment and the Temple and setting up a different sort of Temple, one based on his body, as some sort of protest gesture, then we are describing a reactive Jesus who is in some way moved by the Temple establishment and the Temple, someone for whom those things have power. And it means that there is something rebellious in what he is doing, something of a shaking of a fist at a wicked other. And of course we will do likewise. Which means that whenever we find ourselves faced with some Temple-equivalent in our Christian lives, then we will see the task as being to set up a rival altar which is 'right' and not weighed down by those awful shepherds who have abandoned their sheep and feed only themselves.

I rather think that Jesus understood perfectly well that to set up a rival altar is merely to re-create a new centre of mimetic fascination which is still tied in to the old centre of mimetic fascination as something in rivalry to it. So what Jesus is setting up is not a new centre of mimetic fascination, but something of no fixed place at all, something which looks like the ongoing undoing of our fascination with a sacred other and thus our becoming free to imagine how we might feed sheep.

In other words the 'New Temple' is not a 'Temple' at all. It is the constant undoing of the human tendency to get sucked in to centres of mimetic fascination, thus having our intellects and imaginations dulled, and the constant opening up of our intellects and imaginations towards the engaging in a new form of shepherding, leading people away from being trapped in sacred structures and forms of behaviour run by stumbling blocks. And this is what Church is.

Let me try and spell this out for us as gay and lesbian people becoming involved in ministry, responding to our Lord's com-

manding invitation: 'Feed my sheep.' If we are to be truly faithful
to our Lord's founding of the divine shepherding, which is the
Church, then one of the things we must let go of is our own
tendency to attribute qualities of 'Temple establishment' to our
own churches. It is not what they say they are, or how they act,
which are our problem, but *our imagination* of what they say they
are and how they act. Because it is not they who are going to
circumscribe what we say or do, but our imagination of who they
are, and the authority which our imagination gives them over our
lives.

This seems to me particularly vital for gay and lesbian people
in ministry, but also for anyone in ministry nowadays. Any healthy
ecclesiology must consider not only the traditional questions of
church order and so on resulting from Christ's foundation of the
Church, but also the structure of desire and imagination in the participants with relation to the sort of institutional life which is their
current church order.

Let me try and make this clear. If we have a model of Jesus
who is not indifferent to the Temple, but who is in rivalry with
it, then we will also see the Pope and the Vatican, if we are
Catholic, or whatever the equivalent is in our denomination, as
occupying the place of Annas, Caiaphas and so on, and we will
attribute to them a power and an authority and a coerciveness
which we can resent, and our imaginations can work full-time
in thinking about how awful they are and how heroic we are in
standing up against them. In fact we will not have left the Temple
at all, to take part in Christ's shepherding, but will still be utterly
locked in to the centre of mimetic fascination, with its draw and
its repulsion, and our sense of being good and bad will be utterly
dependent on it.

And here I would like to make a point which is easy to make
as a Catholic, but I hope that you will find ways of translating it
into your own denominational understanding. The point of the
Pope and the Vatican is not that it is the Temple, but that it is
Peter. And the whole point of Peter is that he is not something
splendid and heroic and imposing, but something weak and
unheroic and vacillating. That is to say, just the sort of person

with whom we cannot maintain real communion unless we learn to like him without paying too much attention to whatever bit of braggadocio he and his groupies have come up with. And we learn to like him not because he's nice or good, but because God has chosen to make God's strength and salvation available to those who are able not to mind being in the company of the unheroic, the vacillating, the weak. And of course it is the unheroic, the vacillating and the weak who behave like bullies, and the stronger we are, the more adult we are, then the happier we are just to let them be and not behave in reaction to them.

In other words, if we read Peter as the Temple, and allow ourselves to get all sucked in to sacred rivalry with him, then we will never grow up, but will always be self-indulgent children needing a love/hate-figure. If on the other hand, we learn to see the Pope as Peter, a fumbling figure trying to work out what to do as the Temple keeps on collapsing around him, rather as we ourselves are trying to do, and not let our over-charged imagination of him 'get to us', then there's a chance that we'll start to be able to see that our developing a ministry doesn't depend on him or his approval at all! We don't need the Temple's authority to develop a shepherding. On the contrary, receiving Christ's heart for his sheep means receiving an authority to develop a shepherding in the midst of the collapse of the Temple. We can trust that if a ministry is from God, it will eventually be found to be in harmony with the universal *ecclesia* which is emerging as those called out of darkness together to share in God's unimaginable light.[11]

Now, what I would like to suggest is that our Lord's instruction 'Feed my sheep' will always and inevitably be given to us within a dynamic of learning to look away from the Temple, and developing a heart for the sheep. Which means that it will always be lived by us within the process of learning a certain sort of indifference to 'Church-as-Temple' and of learning a growing sense of affection for what I would call 'Shepherding with Peter', whoever your Peter is.

---

11. Cf. 1 Pet. 2:9.

It is from within this process that we will find ourselves actually able to imagine something new for the sheep whom we have been told to feed. It will be new because our imaginations will not in fact be locked into producing something in reaction to what we think of as 'Temple', and will begin to be being opened out to having a heart for the sheep. And that is what this is all about. I would contend that we know of no heart-for-the-sheep, and can receive no heart-for-the-sheep that does not also come into being through our undergoing the process of detoxifying our patterns of desire with relation to the 'old sacred' and its imagined institutional structures.

If you want to see what I mean, then try this thought experiment for yourselves. And, if you need to, please translate this thought experiment out of Catholic language and into the terms of reference of your own denomination. Just imagine that the Holy Father were to die, something which will happen sometime, one supposes (rather against the evidence); that all the cardinals get together to elect his successor, and that during the conclave there is a virulent outbreak of influenza in Rome which kills off all the cardinals, and all the Vatican employees and a whole lot of others as well. Suddenly they aren't there.

What would this mean? How would you deal with it? Would you be able to imagine yourself reacting as though this incident had no religious significance at all as regards the continuation of the Christian Church? Or would you be plunged either into deep mourning or hysterical rejoicing, or a strange mixture of both? If you were to be gripped with the mixture of mourning and rejoicing, then of course you are seriously tied in to the Temple. If the incident were to have no significance for you at all, then it is because you are already imagining what it is up to *you* to be doing in order to feed God's sheep, and you knew perfectly well before this influenza epidemic that ever since Jesus' death there is no longer a sacred centre, no longer an approving regard of a sacred establishment which you need in order to feel OK about what you are doing.

It is a good thing to do to conduct the experiment of imagining that there is no mimetic centre of fascination any longer, and therefore that shepherding is up to you – if only because as we start to imagine that, we may realise how utterly dependent we are on approval from the other, on being told that I am OK, on feeling that I have a career path, and so on. And then we may get to realise that 'Feed my sheep' is something that can only be done in the midst of the collapse of all that, of all the way I have allowed my imagination to be tied in to something.

Then, as you start to realise that it is all up to you, that Rome, the cardinals, the pope, the Vatican, the bishops and so on, are dead to you, you might find yourself able to begin to re-imagine them not as a sacred burden of approval or disapproval weighing down on you, but as brothers on the same level as you, making available a gift to you, more or less incompetently to be sure, as you are seeking to make available a gift to others.

Now please notice something about this word 'gift'. We can hear it as another disguised form of burden. But supposing that the other which is Church is other to us not as 'sacred temple' but as gift, then that of course means that we can take from it what we perceive to be good,[12] and receive what we need to receive, and sometimes just be grateful for the offer, but take a rain check. But we can also be aware that such and such a thing is not helpful, and yet not get annoyed with those who try to give it a little too insistently – that insistent giving is their problem, not ours. It means that if we disagree with something, then what we are doing is – disagreeing! Which is what adults do, helpfully, within a project for which they share responsibility. This is not dissenting, which is what subordinates do within a project where the responsibility is always with the higher-ups. And there are as we know, but rarely remember, no subordinates in the shepherding, 'For you are all siblings.'[13]

This seems to me to be very important for us now, as we begin to find ourselves free to imagine what it is that we would like to do for our gay and lesbian brothers and sisters, what forms of shepherding we would like to invent for them, how we are to

12. 'Test all things and hold fast to what is good' (1 Thess. 5:21).
13. Matt. 23:8.

receive the heart of Christ for them in concrete practical forms, aware that it depends on us, and that it is a kind of crazy joy to be free to create such things. In order for us to be free to be bold and creative, I think we need to learn how to re-imagine Church as 'gift of shepherding along with Peter in the midst of the collapsing Temple', and not 'coercive Temple whose approval we are condemned to seek, and whose impositions we are condemned to resent'.

Resentment is a pattern of desire such that someone is much more occupied with the obstacle to their project than with the project itself. The sign of grace is when someone finds that their desire has been reformed, so that what had seemed like an obstacle becomes relatively indifferent, and they are ever freer to open up a new and creative project. The difference is that between the pattern of desire which creates suicide bombers and that which creates ministers of the Gospel.

So I ask you to share in my prayer, that 'the mountain be cast into the depths of the sea', the fear be lifted from all our hearts and that we may develop the daring, viscerally moved, shepherdly heart of love[14] along with the creative projects such a heart will enflame as we follow our Lord outside the camp.[15]

---

14. Mark 6:34 and parallels.
15. Heb. 13:13.

the strangeness of this passivity . . .

It is one of the oddest things when something you have read about and 'know about', and vaguely assumed to be true, without giving it too much attention, turns out in fact to *be* true. And especially, of course, when it turns out that it is, as true, something quite unrecognisable in terms of what it looked like when you read about it or 'knew about' it.

Something like this has been my experience in the last eighteen months or so with relation to what I learnt, and I imagine that many others did too, about the supposed difference between ancient and medieval theology, on the one hand, and modern theology on the other. Ancient and medieval theology, we were taught, had a theocentric view of things, in which things came from God to humans, and God was the measure of all things. Modern theology, it is sometimes said, has an anthropocentric view in which humans are the measure of all things; and human subjectivity and the 'turn to the first person' are the necessary starting point in any theological understanding, and thus, I suppose, in any contemplative life.

A good example of the ancient and medieval view would be Aquinas, whose *Summa Theologiae* is taken (and I don't dispute this) to have a view of the things of God, apparently a Neoplatonic view, which is marked by the movement out from God and back to God, with us, as part of the universe of creatures, somewhere on the receiving end: going out from God and coming back to God.

Well, in a sense, all I want to do here is explore the strangeness of having discovered that this so-called 'ancient' view is true. I don't particularly find the Neoplatonic formula of things coming out from God and returning back to God to be helpful. It sounds too tidy, not open-ended enough. But I know what it means. It is the ultimate shift in perception. And it has been dawning on me gradually over the last eighteen months or so, in a sense that is other than merely intellectual. To put it briefly, it is the sense that the real subject of the universe, the world, and of my life, is God. And thus the gradual appreciation that, without in any way being diminished as an acting subject myself, in other words, without any sense of being any the less real a subject for that,[1] time and time again 'I' find myself more properly the subject of passive verbs than of active ones.

I've managed to find three references in St Paul to this sense, and there may be others, but I shall give you these before attempting to look at what the shift means in four different fields of our contemplative life. The first Pauline reference, in chronological order, is Galatians 4:9. Paul is expressing astonishment at how some of his converts, who have received the Spirit of God's Son, could have turned back to their former ways:

> Formerly, when you did not know God, you were in bondage to beings that by nature are no gods; but now that you have come to know God, or rather to be known by God, how can you turn back again to the weak and beggarly elemental spirits, whose slaves you want to be once more?[2]

It is an apparent aside: 'you have come to know God, *or rather to be known by God*'. That is what I am trying to get across. Paul is clearly referring to something new which his converts came to know about God, and that 'coming to know' is better described as a coming to be known.

The second and third references are both in the First Letter to the Corinthians:

---

1. And thus without in any way 'going back on' the 'turn to the self' of modern theology.
2. Gal. 4:8–9.

> Now concerning food offered to idols: we know that "all of us possess knowledge." "Knowledge" puffs up, but love builds up. If any one imagines that he knows something, he does not yet know as he ought to know. But if one loves God, one is known by him.[3]

The contrast here appears to be between knowledge as something held possessively, and the sort of knowledge which comes with love, which is a certain sort of being known, and more like being possessed than possessing.

The third reference is:

> When I was a child, I spoke like a child, I thought like a child, I reasoned like a child; when I became a man, I gave up childish ways. For now we see in a mirror dimly, but then face to face. Now I know in part; then I shall know even as I am known. So faith, hope, love abide, these three; but the greatest of these is love.[4]

In other words, St Paul simply takes it for granted that 'being known' is what underlies all our knowing, and that we do not yet know properly because our 'being known' is still to some extent veiled from us in a world run by rivalry and death. And this 'being known' is in fact the reception of a loving regard towards which we, like so many heliotropes, find ourselves empowered to stretch in faith and hope. No wonder love is the greatest of these three, because it is the coming towards us of what really and inalterably *is*, the regard which creates, while faith and hope are the given response from within us to what is; the given response which love calls forth, while we are 'on the way'. Faith and hope are a relaxing into our being uncovered, discovered, as someone loved. But they are relaxing into love's discovery of us.

---

3. 1 Cor. 8:1–3.
4. 1 Cor. 13:11–13. I have altered the RSV here – it seems to me that the KJV is more accurate, 'known' better than 'understood', and in the absence of an aorist passive in English 'am known' is better than the past perfect 'have been known' which implies an action brought to an end in the past.

What did the treasure in the field think after the man had found it, and covered it over and while he had gone off to sell everything in order to buy the field?[5] Treasure doesn't think, you may say. Precisely. Hence the importance of faith and hope: faith and hope are what it looks like for unthinking treasure, which has no idea of its worth, to find itself actually being able to share in the delight of the one who has found it while waiting for him to come back and take possession. Faith and hope are the contagion from the other's delight in knowing and discovering us, and of course the treasure depends entirely on that never-to-be-withdrawn delight and discovery emanating from the other rather than on anything within itself.

Well, I'd like to see if I can explore what it seems inadequate to call the strangeness of this passivity by sharing some exploratory notes about four different fields: that of psychology, that of the understanding of salvation, that of the life of prayer, and that of living in a world of violence, to see if any of this makes sense.

psychology

One of the ways I knew about this strange passivity 'intellectually' before knowing it 'as finding myself swimming in it' was through the understanding of desire which I set out in Chapter 1 of this book. This is Girard's central insight, and to my mind *the* incalculably important philosophical insight which he has theorised for us. I am talking about the simple, and never-sufficiently-to-be-meditated-on perception, that humans desire according to the desire of another; or, to put it in slightly more literary terms: we receive ourselves through the eyes of another.

All I want to say is that this is not a metaphor, but, I take it, a simple and apt anthropological description of how any of us comes to be. Let me try and set the scene appropriately: someone important comes into the room, a room in which a group of

---

5. Matt. 13:44: "The kingdom of heaven is like treasure hidden in a field, which a man found and covered up; then in his joy he goes and sells all that he has and buys that field."

people are gathered, among whom you are. This is someone important whom you have been expecting, and for whose recognition you have been hoping. Now when that person comes in, your feeling, sense of worth and so on will depend entirely on her recognition of you. Will she notice me? If she does notice me, will it be with clear pleasure? Will she come over to me? Or will I be to her simply as another anonymous figure who happens to be present? This, I would say, is not something of which you are necessarily conscious, still less do you formulate it. In fact you will pick it up in your body. If her body language is clearly relaxed and pleased to see you, any smile she gives you will be picked up by your body as communicating that pleasure, and you will feel an uplift, your spirit will soar, and you will have the sense 'Yes, I really *am*.' If, on the other hand, whatever her smile says, her body language indicates that she is going through the motions, being polite, wants to be somewhere else, that you are not really important to her, then your body will pick it up, and in the dawning disappointment, part of your self will slink yelping away like a wounded puppy, tail between the legs.

Now the way that our sense of self is given to us through the eyes of another is not simply a function of adult behaviour, as I hope is obvious. It is what we are inducted into being from the moment we were conceived. The other is always massively prior to us, and we are always in fact being drawn in, from our vulnerable infancy onwards, as peripheral to something anterior to us, whether that other is physical existence, language, memory, or sense of self. We are drawn in through repeated infantile sound and gesture, and it is imitation that gives us being. We always come to inhabit what is other than us, a health system, an education system, a country, a cultural and linguistic field of reference, as massively the recipient of something rather than its protagonist in any dramatic way.

If this is true, then in the case of any of us, our 'I', rather than being the fixed point from which our desire and our understanding flow, is the malleable symptom of that which is prior to, and other than, us. We are participatory 'symptoms', as it were, who become what we are in the flow of what is prior to us and gives us being, and in both our receiving of that being and our denial of that reception do we come to be. Which is why any insistence on *my* originality, on the priority of *my* desires, or of *my* ideas, can in fact so easily cut me off from being a recipient, and turn me into one who reacts against, which is always the high route to smallness of spirit and weakness of creativity. I wonder whether our most creative musicians and writers haven't in fact been those who were most easily able to sit loose to their own extraordinary capacity to suck in the playing cards around them, shuffle them and deal them out again in a series of new juxtapositions which gave their contemporaries a sense of extraordinary novelty. Only someone like Rossini, who wasn't in competition with Mozart, could so happily and recognisably borrow bits of Mozart as jokes in his own music and yet manifestly be producing something entirely his own. And it is only the glance from posterity which can see how much any of these 'original geniuses' was original not in creating something *ex nihilo*, but in throwing up with delight that in which they were swimming, as though it swam within *them*.

The point of this is that St Paul is not making some arcane or mystical point in talking about the essential Christian discovery as being one of being known by God. On the contrary, he is showing some of the first fruits of the extraordinary anthropological discovery about who we really are which came into our ken in the wake of Jesus' resurrection. If the true other who is prior to all of us is absolutely not on the same level as all the rivalries, fears, acts of possession, and creations of identity over against each other, then the emergence of that other destabilises what we took to be our self by making available to us a capacity to relax into being called into being without having to forge a being over against the other. We can be happy to ride being a 'symptom' of another's causality rather than fearing that unless we can somehow make it into being the cause, we will fall out of being.

In other words, the other who is prior to us is not in rivalry with us, and we don't need to possess who we are as though we would lose it if we didn't grab it. There is not a scarcity of being or of regard from the other, against which we need to protect ourselves. And so we find ourselves being discovered and known in just the same sense as a really first-rate impresario spots a talented future actor or singer long before the actor or singer knows that they are really talented, 'have what it takes'. And it is in the impresario believing in them that they are able to be discovered. They were 'known' before they knew it. And if we were to be such an actor or singer saying 'I was discovered', we wouldn't merely mean that someone with the right connections had simply lighted upon our talent, which was already there. We would mean that their act of knowing, of discovering was actually creative of something into being. Our talent would be in some kind a symptom of their discovery of us.

So, the important person coming into the room turns out to be not on her way somewhere else, not harassed at having to deal with all the people who are seeking her attention, desperate for her acknowledgement; not miserly with her regard. On the contrary, she enters the room with full deliberation and has come in to stay, and her regard does indeed give you and me the sense that we are being discovered, that we are being invited to participate in something much bigger than ourselves, in which we will find that there is a real 'me' there to be known, one that we could scarcely imagine before. The body language of this important person speaks as completely as her words, its relaxedness, unhurriedness and serenity are quite simply what real deliberateness and power look like, and are picked up as such.

To shift key slightly, but only very slightly: what would it look like to imagine the Eucharist as the body language of God come into our midst? Wouldn't it be simply – accurate?

understanding salvation

This brings us from psychology to the understanding of salvation. More than anything else over the last years, in which I have found myself talking about redemption and forgiveness to different groups of people, I have found that the shift which is required for sense to emerge is exactly the same as the one I have been describing. Any account of our salvation at the hands of Jesus which is a description of something which happened, or happens, but told as if by a spectator or an onlooker, is fatally flawed. And what is fatally flawed about it is that it is not told as an undergoing of something which is happening to me and which is turning me into a different sort of teller.

In other words, it is not being told by someone who is funda-mentally passive to, patient of, something enormous happening which includes them and which is actually altering not only the words they say, but their capacity to be uttering words at all. For when we talk of salvation, rather than describing something happening 'out there' we are in fact allowing ourselves to be 'con-taminated' by what we perceive in and behind the regard of one coming towards us. Let me try to illustrate this.

A straight friend of mine from South America wrote back to me after reading the chapter on the Gerasene demoniac in my book *Faith beyond Resentment* to tell me what a revelation it had been for him. It had brought back to him a series of incidents when he was at secondary school. He and his classmates had lighted upon the class 'maricón', the class 'fairy', and had teased and bullied this guy remorselessly. Eventually the pupil in question had managed, no doubt after much beseeching his parents, to go off somewhere else, to another part of Venezuela, and my friend described to me how completely bereft he and his classmates had been left by this guy's absence, how they had found themselves lost as a group without their class 'maricón'. So, not apparently needing to read Girard in order to understand what to do next, they managed to find another class fairy in a different class, and settled on him instead, and so shored up their group.

It had come as a revelation to my friend, some years later, that this is what he had been doing. And I imagine indeed that he was engaged in that persecution in all 'innocence', not knowing what he was doing. But I do not suppose that all the pupils in the group were equally ignorant of what they were doing. I suspect that the members of the group who would find it most difficult to analyse what they had been doing in the same clear and clean way as my friend did would be precisely those who had experienced some sense of relief *at the time* with respect to the treatment of the class fairy *'because it was not me'*. In other words, someone else was occupying the place of shame, and I am deeply relieved that it is they and not I who am there, half-aware how arbitrary it is that it should be they and not I. And that means that whereas some people in the group, who are less insecure in their own status as 'one of the lads', don't really attribute much importance to the creation of the victim, just going along with it, there are others whose contribution to the building up of group membership over against the class 'fairy' is, let us say, motivated by a curious personal enthusiasm, who have developed let us say, firmer reasons than most for considering the other guy to be 'evil' or 'not one of us'.

Now, let us suppose that our class 'fairy' suddenly comes back to the school from elsewhere in Venezuela, free, happy, with no sense of revenge, delighted to see his former classmates. Let us begin to imagine what it is like to be in their shoes. Especially for those who were to some extent half-aware of how important it was *for them* that this guy occupied the place he had in their own constellation of emotional and social life, the return of the class fairy might be seriously destabilising. If he came back breathing threats and vengeance, that wouldn't be so destabilising, because he would still be occupying the place of shame which they had given him, but would be merely occupying it as one trying to turn the tables with an inversion of strength. But if he comes back entirely free of vengefulness, and with no desire to turn tables on anybody, this is much more destabilising *because it completely removes the place of shame*. The person who can occupy the place of shame without caring what the group thinks of him is of course a particular threat to those who have most at stake in maintaining the group identity, which is to say, those for whom the place of shame is felt to be something close to them, something that they especially fear to occupy themselves, and thus for whom the enthusiasm with which they keep alive the group structure is strongest and most personally felt.

We can imagine how some of these people might be not at all pleased to see their former class fairy back if he was free of revenge, and thus, from their point of view, in contempt of their sacred order. It is the pits of their stomachs above all which will feel him as a threat. That is step one in my reconstruction: something happened that was destabilising, and is perceived to have something to do 'with me' in exactly the degree to which I am bound in, with greater or lesser awareness, into both needing a place of shame, and also needing to avoid being the person who occupies that place. The 'Other' is just there, as destabilising.

Step two is the perception, which dawns gradually, that the other is not there, occupying this space, by accident. It is as if it begins to dawn that the class fairy was perfectly deliberately occupying that space in the first place. It's not just that he 'got over' the awful treatment which he received, thus putting into doubt the ability of the awful treatment to create, sustain and define a world. Far worse than that. It begins to become apparent that he had chosen freely to occupy that space and for a very curious reason: he knew how much the class needed there to be a place of shame in order for them to feel good; yet he also knew what a terrible diminishment of any of their capacity to be free and happy the need for that sort of group belonging leads to; and he decided to occupy the 'place of shame' himself, not so as to attract attention to himself, not even 'as a substitute', letting someone else off the hook, but with a far richer project in mind than that. He wanted to create the possibility that people he liked should be able to live free and happy without a place of shame and without ever needing to create one again.

Here we are beginning to come to grasp that strange passivity once again. What salvation looks like is the perception of a hugely powerful loving project as having come towards us and caught us unawares, where we fitted him into our scheme, unaware that he was deliberately occupying that place in our scheme so as to let us off having to live in a way run by such schemes. In other words, we thought we were in control, but we weren't. And what is bizarre, and destabilising, and perhaps the most difficult thing to grasp about the Good News is that we have not been 'caught out' by someone who *confronts* us. What has been 'caught out' is the unreal, fear-bound 'we' which we took to be the real we. But the one coming towards us is not coming towards us in the first instance as a confrontation. Much more bizarre and slower to develop than this is our perception that in order to have decided to come among us at all, and to occupy our place of shame, he must actually have really known and liked us all along.

Just try to think what it means for a violent man to discover that the object of his violence liked him before, during and after the violence, and had placed himself before him not in order to confront him, but because he knew perfectly well that the violent man was subject to a compulsion, and he longed for the violent man to be free. The realisation that the one who seemed to be my object was in fact a presence of far, far greater strength than I, and that I was in fact, all along, the object of that person's entirely friendly, knowing regard – this, I think, is what leads to the strange passivity which I have described. 'I' am undone and I am discovered as known in the as-yet-unimagined regard of another.

This is also why I think that there is no Christian discourse of any sort at all that is not one undergoing this loss of 'I' and the being discovered with a new 'I'. And I think that this is exactly what we mean when we say 'I believe in the forgiveness of sins'. What I think is meant by that phrase from our Creed is: 'It is as "being forgiven", as undergoing, finding myself strangely passive, towards someone who is unbinding my previous way of belonging that I am given to believe in one who knows and loves me.'

And this power of another, lovingly taking away the place of shame and our dependence on it, can be resisted. Ever since the Gospel was first preached it has been possible to refuse the consequences of God occupying the place of shame, thus rendering it null, so that there is no longer a place of shame. It has been possible to insist on trying to maintain a place of shame, on re-creating one, on refusing the collapse of the sacred. And this has led to families being against each other, children against parents and vice versa. This is why the one who inaugurated it knew that he would bring not peace but a sword, but also why he knew that once done, it could not be undone, and that fighting against it is futile, sad and irrelevant. Sad for those caught up in it, because it is the definition of that which cannot be forgiven, since it is what refusing the offering of forgiveness looks like. This necessarily puts into question all our mechanisms for controlling forgiveness, which means, for ring-fencing the place of shame, which is why it is religious professionals who are the most greatly at risk[6] since it is so easy for us to re-create a place of shame, making it seem that we have the power of forgiveness, rather than finding ourselves caught up as multipliers of the divine annulment of the place of shame. But this is irrelevant, something rather like blowing against a hurricane.[7] There is no place of shame, and all attempts to re-create it partake of futility, refuse to dwell in the strange passivity of being brought to fullness of creation.

prayer

So much for our understanding of salvation. Now for prayer. Supposing what I have said about the strangeness of passivity is true, then the principal place where we undergo both the strangeness and the passivity is prayer. It is not true that we pray so as to move God. It is truer that in our praying God is moving us. It is truer that we are prayed-in than that we pray.[8] This I take to be absolutely in line with Paul's teaching in Romans: 'Likewise the Spirit helps us in our weakness; for we do not know how to pray as we ought, but the Spirit himself intercedes for us with sighs too deep for words.'[9] It is also, surely, the point of our Lord's insistence:

> "And in praying do not heap up empty phrases as the Gentiles do; for they think that they will be heard for their many words.

---

6. Cf. Matt. 12:31–2.
7. Some versions of Acts 9:5 have the risen Lord saying to Saul, "I am Jesus whom you are persecuting; it is hard for you to kick against the goads." This is the power of one who likes the one who has been caught up in being violent towards him, and is even affectionately sorry for him that he is having such a hard time being a persecutor. It is the affection which is really destabilising!
8. Cf. Herbert McCabe, *God Still Matters* (London: Continuum, 2002), Chs. 5 and 6.
9. Rom. 8:26.

Do not be like them, for your Father knows what you need before you ask him.''[10]

If it is true that our 'self' is a symptom, then prayer is God's way of getting into the symptom from within and transforming it. This picture of the self does indeed presuppose that we don't really know what we want, a discovery which may be one of the most important things about learning to pray. And this means not that we can't make our mind up about this desire or that desire, but that our mind is made up of, constituted by, contradictory desires such that we can't desire in a healthy way at all. The reason why our Lord insists on prayer is not so as to turn us all into mystics who levitate and float off walls, though that would be fun too, but because it is by agreeing to get in touch with, and not mind sitting with and in the contradictory, somewhat 'smelly' desires which move us that we are able to allow our desire to be strengthened, directed, ordered, so that we actually become someone. This is the promise of prayer: don't be content with too little, dare to be given to become someone. And the promise is realised as a resting in and trusting in one who 'knows what you need before you ask him' which means, who is the active subject whose 'symptom' you are.

This picture is, of course, perfectly clear to people from an animist culture, since the idea of them being possessed by, and then moved by, a spirit which comes down upon them and gives them to be someone else is perfectly obvious. The malleability of selfhood is taken for granted. The picture of course is quite right, but the possessing Spirit about which I am talking is on quite a different level from Ogum or Oxalá, Pomba Gira or Sete Capas, to name some of the 'spirits' which 'come down' on people in the Afro-Brazilian cults. Those spirits offer a temporary (and sometimes violent) displacement of 'self'. But being possessed by the Holy Spirit is different because, since it is the Spirit of God who is not in rivalry with us, it can move us and re-create us without displacing us. But we would do well to remember that

10. Matt. 6:7–8.

we, just like the participants in those cults, are those who by prayer are learning to sit loose to becoming possessed by a new Spirit, who are being broken in by a new horse.

We use the word 'indwelt' to signify the peacefulness of this particular possession, because we are possessed by someone who is not in rivalry with us, but who gradually gives us to be what we find we were always meant to be, such that we are not simply passive in a straightforward sense, as is someone who is in a trance. Part of that person has to go to sleep in order for the temporary aberration to take over. We are passive in that we find that our becoming entirely active, and indeed entirely free-acting agents, is something given to us as we learn to have our resisting undone. A wind displaces a sailing boat which moves before it, but the fire of the Spirit warms the air which makes a hot-air balloon free and mobile from within. The experience of prayer is that of the gradual learning to rejoice in my induction by an entirely gentle, trust-worthy power, into freedom from all my ways of being tied in to the place of shame, one by one, and discovering this as given to me as a 'real me' in a series of new desires for new projects which share the huge affection and gentleness towards others that I have found myself receiving.

living in a world of violence

I would like to end by being very tentative about something which has exercised me considerably over the last year or so, and this is to do with what the sort of 'indifference' looks like, the sort of 'turning away', the sort of refusal to be 'fascinated' by wars, rumours of wars and revolutions which our Lord advocated, and which I highlighted in Chapter 1. This indifference, this turning away emerged as Our Lord laid bare the structure of a satanic world order, and the 'pseudo events' which that structure regu-larly produces in the hopes of keeping us on board. And I take it that as we learn to see through his eyes, we are learning to see with the eyes of the Creator who is coming towards us.

We have all been living these last several months under wars and rumours of wars. And I think I need to make a distinction between two sorts of passivity which we must work hard not to confuse. There is the sort of passivity which is induced by what I might call 'lies-and-violence fatigue'. It is a kind of attitude of 'a plague on both your houses, I am going to cultivate my garden' which is produced by the sheer volume of the barrage of lies and the distortions of power which emanate from the US government, our own government and that of others in the Middle East and elsewhere. Maybe part of the effect of this is to bludgeon us into a sense of helplessness. It is how helplessness is normalised into us.

This is, I think, the wrong sort of passivity. It is the passivity of those being ground down. It is a distraction and a dulling, a diminution of life, of interest, of zest. The strangeness of the passivity which I am out to try and point to is that, in receiving it, I become able to take all that violence and disturbance for granted, as so much froth in the midst of which we find ourselves being allowed to glimpse something which is huge and peaceful and gentle and being brought into being. Something which is simply unable to be perceived by those who are frightened that unless they do something, they will not be. Unless they achieve something, or provoke something, there will be nothing.

But we find ourselves undergoing contagion at the hand of One who is bringing things into being, who is drawing close with a power, a serenity and a purpose in the light of which all the apparently 'meaning-giving events' are distractions and in whose approaching light we are already being enabled to resist being driven by all that casting around for meaning, that dangerous need to be good. The New Testament is full of the language of perseverance, of patience, of being found standing. It is also full of the language of non-resistance. In fact we are told *not to* resist evil in human form, but indeed *to* resist the devil. The distinction is interesting. For in anthropological terms it is exactly the same thing *to* resist human evil and *not to* resist the devil. Just as it is exactly the same thing *not to* resist human evil, and *to* resist the devil. Resisting human evil off our own bat is how we create Satanic meaning by becoming part of an endless tit for tat. Refusing to resist evil is how we refuse to create Satanic meaning, and how we are given to find ourselves taking part in the creation of real meaning, which is to say, in creation which is coming upon us from Another.

I find myself resisting the clear implication of this: part of me wants to say 'Yes, this stuff about passivity is all very well, but of course you can't just trust God and turn your back on what's going on.' Indeed not. The sort of passivity I'm referring to is finding myself given to be an active subject in another project whose parameters are not defined by 'putting things right'. In the dwelling in this project, there may be moments when it looks as though I am entirely dedicated to combating a particular evil, rather than brushing it off on my way somewhere else, but if that really is the case, I will have been seduced out of the project in return for too fickle a meaning, too trite a glory. My resistance is, I suspect, a wanting to eat my cake and have it. I suspect that I am resisting the loss of apparent moral relevancy, a relevancy which is kept going if one keeps one foot in the camp of those commentators who create new meanings out of fast-changing current events. And I suspect that I know that my game is up: I will lose moral relevancy, and will discover instead that I am being carried off into someone who likes me, to take part in creation with them, and I will love it.

Chapter One is a modified version of a talk given in Downside Abbey in November 2001. It has appeared in *The Merton Journal* Vol. 9 No. 1 (Easter 2002), and is published here by kind permission of the Editor.

Chapters Two, Three and Four were originally planned as a triptych, though they came into being under very different circumstances.

Chapters Two and Three were prepared for the meeting of the Irish Theological Association held in Dublin in March 2002.

Chapter Four is a modified translation of a talk given in the Universidad Iberoamericana in Mexico City in April 2002.

Chapter Five is a modified version of a talk given to the British and Irish Association for Practical Theology in Durham in July 2002. It has appeared in *The Way* Vol. 42 No. 1 (January 2003), and is published here by kind permission of the Editor.

Chapter Six saw the light of day as a Millennium Lecture given at the Parish of St Joseph's in the Village in New York City in May 2002.

Chapter Seven is a modified version of a talk given to Quest, the UK group for Lesbian and Gay Catholics, in London Colney in July 2002.

Chapter Eight is a modified version of a talk given for the Center of Lesbian and Gay Studies at the Pacific School of Religion, part of the Graduate Theological Union, at Berkeley, California in September 2002

Chapter Nine is a modified version of a talk given for The Thomas Merton Society in London in October 2002. It appeared in *The Merton Journal* Vol. 10 No. 2 (Easter 2003) and is published here by kind permission of the Editor.

INDEX